D0912069

A LLŶN ANTHOLOGY

A Llŷn
Anthology

Edited by
Dewi Roberts

Prologue by
Jim Perrin

First published in 2008

© Text: Dewi Roberts

Published with the financial support
of the Welsh Books Council

ISBN: 978-1-84527-172-5

Cover design: Sian Parri

Published by Gwasg Carreg Gwalch,
12 Iard yr Orsaf, Llanrwst, Wales LL26 0EH
☎ 01492 642031
🖷 01492 641502
✆ books@carreg-gwalch.co.uk
Internet: www.carreg-gwalch.co.uk

for Ruth Bidgood
in friendship

Contents

Introduction

The singular eye of the creative writer can skillfully evoke the spirit of place and focus on facets of a region which we might tend to take for granted for much of the time. The poet and the prose writer can throw a fresh and unexpected perspective on a landscape and its people and also illuminate historical facets. I find this to be abundantly true of Llŷn, Eifionydd and Ynys Enlli.

The geographical shape of the peninsula has been compared to a dragon's tail, an apt metaphor in a country where the flag which bears the red image of this mythical creature is a colourful reminder of its prestigious past.

As hinted above, in order to enhance both the interest and the length of the anthology, I have gone beyond the boundaries of Llŷn.

The main emphasis has been to include purely literary material. However, it would be difficult to work on a book of this kind and exclude some historical accounts.

As the reader turns the pages he, or she, will move from the Mesolithic period to the age of the saints and, much later, learn something of the rivalry which developed between Porthdinllaen and Holyhead over the establishment of a packet service to Ireland. To bring us a little more up to date Jan Morris writes of the gallant sabotage of part of a site which had been acquired by the RAF as a bombing school. The three distinguished men who were convicted were forced to take the action they did in an attempt to preserve the heritage of Llŷn, its language, culture and ideals.

Today the Welsh language learning centre at Nant Gwrtheyrn is making a major contribution to the preservation of the language, as a poem in these pages by Mike Jenkins testifies.

At Llanystumdwy, Tŷ Newydd, the writers' centre for Wales, in Lloyd George's former home, has established a high reputation and motivated me towards a career as writer and editor.

11

Various genres of writing will be found in these pages, and Welsh language writers in translation are included as well as Welsh writers in English. In addition a number of English writers are represented.

The book is intended as a celebration of one of the most beautiful parts of the British Isles, and I am grateful to Jim Perrin for setting the tone of things to come in his inspirational prologue.

Dewi Roberts

Note: Original spellings of place-names in certain pieces have been retained.

Prologue: The Margins

In cities that
have outgrown their promise people
are becoming pilgrims
again, if not to this place,
then to the recreation of it
in their own spirits.

R. S. Thomas, 'The Moon in Llŷn'

Mercury columns of rain glanced with sunshine swayed and drifted in across the sea as we slipped down from the coastal path, out of the gale and into little Porth Iago, most secretive of bays in Llŷn. Refracted light caught at and blanched our footsteps into sand wet from a retreating tide. We crossed to the farther wall of rock, rested there in the calm below the storm with the wind sighing and roaring above like a beast frustrated of its prey, then crept into the fractal mimicry of a sheltering crevice-cove. On its miniature dry strand, in still air, we huddled in our waterproofs, sat close, lit our meths stove, filled the kettle, waited for splutter of spout, clack of lid – all that happy, quiet ritual the trivial preoccupations of which ease the mind of care. And we indulged ourselves in good, ground, strong coffee, passed the mug between us, sweet liquid on our lips, watched quietly, looked around . . .

A flight of six cormorants struggled in awkwardly from the north, stiff-winged, veering this way and that, craning their necks to find leads through air that was buffeting and solid as water. A solitary raven in virtuoso display tumbled and careened nearby, watchful, respectful, as though a basilisk glare from the sea-hags might turn him to dropping stone. One of them looked towards him, wings labouring, and then, losing ground in the ragged formation, looked away. Two choughs fluttered and screamed. An oystercatcher scurried and piped. The peregrine of Pen y Cil swept past briefly, imperiously, and the sun emerging from under cloud turned a kestrel's wings to flame. Ah, these spirits of the place, and us at our observances, silent, sipping our coffee, the mug going from hand to hand; communion wine, 'the place of Angels and the Gate of Heaven'.

So the light had come and we looked for it in the waves as they drew themselves up, unrolling sheets of milky ultramarine, balancing their careering crests tenuously into the slant of the light; so that they became lapis lazuli infused and set with gold brilliance, intensity, cascading prisms. Here one swirled sand across the palette, streaking itself ochre; the tempest-gust caught at another and gave us sudden, flung diamonds. Such riches . . .

The rain has ceased, I watch this lovely, slender woman cross the strand, see the wind spin the red-gold of her hair into a net to catch the sun. She picks up a great rope of seaweed and, strong shoulders bending to the task, she sketches all across the empty canvas of the beach, like a child dancing in the wind, playful and skittish as the raven above her. Then she crosses to the other, needled wall of the cove. Pre-Cambrian. Was this the first stilling out of the magma? Again that fractal sense. I struggle with scale. Aiguilles? The Cuillin? All miniature here, but somehow the same. The overall cast is sombre, until you look closely ('the World is a mirror of infinite beauty, yet no man sees it'.) So much colour here: a washed-out purple that the powdery grey of limpets and barnacles shows off to perfection; there are creased and pillowy crags frilled with salt-crystals where the spray reaches; what definition can words give to the greens and blues that I see, to the shapes and forms, to the seamed quartz crosses like spirit-kisses from the grain of the cliff? And the waves surge continually, and the light is a strange, gold, slantwise suffusion of air, my loved one dancing and I very still, without property here, heart wide open . . .

'If we see things as they are, then we do not have to interpret or analyze them further; we do not need to try to understand things by imposing spiritual experience or philosophical ideas upon them.'

Yet in this old, far-off region of Llŷn is a texture that calls to the questing mind, produces a tension there. We are close to the margins: of land, of a country. Wales, country of those the Saxons termed the Weallas – the foreigners – westernmost, west – is it a mood, a feeling, a need, a cultural and historical entity as well as all this exquisite physical fabric we see? I have felt this complex atmosphere in so many places of the West: on Beara out in West Cork; by the shore of dark Loch Hourn, looking across to Ladhar Bheinn on Knoydart; in the silky machair along the seaward side of sacred Iona. Maybe here, rooted in the actuality of these landscapes, is the locating, the embodiment of a concept complementary to what we understand as East (from whence the wisdom of that last quotation). Surely it is as meaningful and valuable, this affective mood-concept, as many from western societies this century have found what the East offers in spiritual, philosophical and cultural terms? In Irish, the word for West is Iar, which means also the end, the extremity, the last thing ('of life, and death, and the last things'). When I think of West, it comes to me in memory's eye as the extreme edge of Europe. Each place mirroring its preceding thought, the tunnel of mind-mirrors takes me back to the last place in which those peoples whose historical moment was concurrent with that of the Roman Empire, and whose migrations began in the Celtic Cradle, fetched up before the impassable ocean.

A sense of historical irony enthralls me: that the relict and exigent cultures which lighted upon these stony coasts flickered here and there into glories, into visions of holy life, into mythopoeic achievement – Columba, Patrick, the Book of Kells – which tantalised and occasionally informed the real barbarism and malevolence which had swept them there (tell Augustine of Canterbury that the monks are still fleeing from the massacre he ordained at Bangor Is-coed). So that ultimately – the dominant and displacing cultures themselves dead or in decay – these rocks and coves and wild sanctuaries transformed and located into places of pilgrimage, means of expiation and escape, refutations of the values of material possession, national supremacy and martial power which had originally marginalised them. Into these places came the fleeing ones, the questing ones, the worshippers and the refuseniks: 'The sea foamed to the beat of hostile oars . . . ice-bound Hibernia wept for the heaps of slain Scots.'

A tenet of Celtic Christianity, as I understand it, is this: to follow sunwise, westwards, perhaps is to take some steps towards the wisdom the access to which is through the loss or abnegation of power; is to apprehend the metaphor implicit both in the sun's slantwise celebration and enlargement of the natural world, and in the greater beauty at its setting than at its zenith. In the reflective fragments of history and culture that still attach to these furthermost places of an old land – Scotland and the Western Isles, the West of Ireland, Wales – are there values to be found by those who come searching for them (and more dangerously, do those who search also at times traduce)? Maybe the structures, contexts and apparent necessities of our 'western' society have marginalised the unsupported living in these places more than ever before, the physical and mental skills of survival have been lost, and here and there the barbarism has leap-frogged through into occupation. But where landscape has imagistic power, where it is a threshold elementally stated – as here, at Porth Iago on this ragged, thrust-out fist of Penllyn – does that shadow-life of historical presence, in its starkness of choice, history and preoccupation, have a potential for spiritual regeneration stronger than in the hinterlands, quickening the imagination? At times I wonder, and I watch the walkers on the coastal paths of the West, and catch at the sense emanating from them of something unstated, unconscious, drawing them there . . .

What journeys would I undertake, where would I go to find out, what deliberate, cumulative and interreactive pattern could I weave to support such a thesis? Would a part of it centre around the locations of an imaginative system –

the Arthurian Cycle – the branch-legends of which are suffused with a sense of West; a system which, whilst historically open to fraud ('Hic iacet Rex quondam Rexque futuris' wrote the scheming monks of Glastonbury), nonetheless aspires in true pilgrim fashion after Grace. Are there to be found – between the inexplicable, the fraudulent and the incomprehensible ('there is so much blindness and ingratitude and damned folly in it,') that even in the loveliest places plague our intellects – moments, locations, where humane values have flourished and may flourish still, as they do not flourish throughout much of our soft-totalitarian state, with its subservience to capital, its desperate need to control, its abject, squeaking fear of difference?

> . . . the brownshirts themselves
> Fear the man whose arm doesn't fly up
> And are terrified of the man who
> Wishes them a good morning.
> The shrill voices of those who give orders
> Are full of fear like the squeaking of
> Piglets awaiting the butcher's knife.

There is a threshold marked out by the recurrent, wavering point in the histories of civilisations where the balance between amelioration and corruption is finely held ('It is a Temple of Majesty, yet no man regards it.'). Maybe in tracing it you hold to the argument for the necessity of pilgrimage ('It is a region of light and peace, did not men disquiet it.'). So I make an effort to give definition to the idea that West, like East, is not only place but also perhaps even a distinctive and therapeutic state of mind – a letting-go, a coming-to-terms with the wilderness within, a celebration of the beauty of wilderness in nature ('It is the Paradise, more to man since he is fallen than it was before'), without which our lives are the more savage. And yet, circumspectly:

> . . . man hath all which Nature hath, but more,
> And in that more lie all his hopes of good.

The tragedy lies in his loss of equilibrium at that wavering point; it lies in the turning to security, the reliance on currency you can grasp and hoard. That gilded wave-crest, those flung diamonds, inexpressible riches – what vault would hold them, and what could they buy?

The storm having passed, we climb out of our sheltering cove. We shall carry on, round over Mynydd Anelog, and arrive at sunset atop the great last headland of Braich y Pwll, a seaward mountain the heather slopes of which keen down into the tide-race, and from whence we shall look across to Ynys Enlli, where the surviving, escaping Bangor monks found refuge – Bardsey, with its lighthouse flashing across in the gathering shades. In looking forward to that view, I think of the last time I left Enlli's harbour, gazing back from the stern of a small boat and seeing a woman on the promontory above holding her yoga pose rigid, angular against the sun, self-consciously, proprietorially, somehow engendering irritation in her assertion of spiritual superiority, her colonising, her pose. There is a materialism of the spirit, too, a possibility of avarice there (tell Saint Dunawd of Bangor-below-the-wood that his well on the pilgrims' way as it toils up from Black Rock is cattle-mired and broken now, unregarded, its water fouled . . .)

> . . . fly our paths, our feverish contact fly!
> For strong the infection of our mental strife,
> Which, though it gives no bliss, yet spoils for rest.

From the path along the cliff-top above Porth Iago I look back down, and in the sand, etched there, an open heart, beyond it the white tide, turning . . .

Jim Perrin

18

Places

Llŷn

I. Clynnog Fawr

All slender Llŷn lay beyond,
reaching westward into rain,
rocking with autumn winds.
That day cold was a presence
in the great empty church.
Easiest to sense, of all
who had come there, were those
who struggled, failed, returned –
the tight-lipped and the weepers,
the hesitant, defective, self-obsessed,
the manic and the ever-doubting;
so that there seemed to rise,
within the thin wind's meagre celebration,
difficult praise from the uncomforted.

II. Aberdaron

From here, only sea-roads
run on.
          We ate and drank
by a streaming window.
From the edge of day
an unstable plain,
grey-green and white,
came tilting, sliding towards us.
High-tide breakers
exploded just below.
I realised how much fear
there is in awe.

But one,
a scholar, she ninety and more,
looked out at the waves
with a friend's acceptance,
and, glass in hand, turned back
to conversation, laughter;
as little daunted by the years,
by journeys or soaking weather,
as by that great uneasy sea.

III. Enlli

Faint and grey, Bardsey came out of the mist.
We could just catch, out there, what a poet saw
seven centuries back: the white waves leaping
around the holy island of Enlli.
No sound from them; the wind was too loud,
and the sea too loud, against the headland,
beating, tearing.

That's how the island
has stayed with me, a far silence
within storm, a shadow hardly seen,
beyond the clarity of gorse on the hill,
and the blurred surging of the autumn sea.

I have never landed there; the place
remains more visitant than friend.
Why it should be so loved, though,
I can sense, unclearly, as I still see
that shape far out in spume and rain,
beyond the silent waves that leap and leap
around the holy island of Enlli.

Ruth Bidgood

Pen Llŷn

Dafydd looked out;
I look out: five centuries
without change? The same sea breaks
on the same shore and is not
broken. The stone in Llŷn
is still there, honey-
coloured for a girl's hair
to resemble. It is time's
smile on the cliff
face at the childishness
of my surprise. Here was the marriage
of land and sea, from whose bickering
the spray rises. 'Are you there?'
I call into the dumb
past, that is close to me
as my shadow. 'Are you here?'
I whisper to the encountered
self like one coming
on the truth asleep
and fearing to disturb it.

R. S. Thomas (1913-2000)

Llŷn

Skies tower here, and we are small.
Winters, we sleep on a flap of land
in a dark throat. We taste the salt
of its swallow. Huge cold breaths
hurtle over, cascade down
till we feel the house hunch.

When morning comes at last
houses sit up with pricked ears
on reefs of land the black tide
leaves, or sidle crab-wise
to the lane, their small squashed faces
giving nothing of their thoughts away.

In summer, flowers loosening with seed
reach out to fingerstroke
cars passing in the long sweet dusk.
Hay-meadows sigh. Pearl-pale
in the bracken on the headland
shorn ewes step delicate
and wary as young unicorns.

The sea we look out over is a navel
the wrinkled belly-button
of an older world: after dark
like busy star-systems, the lights
of Harlech, Aberystwyth, Abergwaun
wink and beckon. The sun's gone down
red as a wound behind Wicklow.
A creaking of sail away
Cernyw and Llydaw wait.

Once, here was where what mattered
happened. A small place
at the foot of cliffs of falling light;

horizons that look empty.
If we let ourselves believe it,
fringes.

Christine Evans

Fires on Llŷn

At sunset we climb Uwchmynydd
to a land's end
where R. S. Thomas walks, finding
the footprint of God
warm in the shoe of the hare.

Words shape-shift to wind, a flight
of oystercatchers,
whinchat on a bush, two cormorants
fast-dipping wings
in a brilliant sea.

Over the holy sound Enlli
is dark in a ruff
of foam. Any pebble or shell
might be the knuckle-bone
or vertebra of a saint.

Three English boys throw stones.
Choughs sound alarm.
Sea-birds rise and twenty thousand saints
finger the shingle
to the sea's intonation.

Facing west, we've talked for hours
of our history,

thinking of Ireland and the hurt
cities,
gunshot on lonely farms,

praised unsectarian saints,
Enlli open
to the broken rosary
of their coracles,
praying in Latin and Welsh.

Done with cliff-talking we turn
inland, thinking
of home silently filling
with shadows, the hearth
quiet for the struck match,

our bed spread with clean sheets.
Our eyes are tired
with sun-gazing. Suddenly
we shout – the farms burn.
Through binoculars we see

distant windows curtained with flame.
The fires are real
that minute while we gasp, begin
to run, then realise
windows catch, not fire but

the setting sun. We are struck still
without a word
in any language. See the hares run,
windows darken,
hear the sea's mumbled novenas.

Gillian Clarke

Incongruous

The pattern of long sandy beaches curving between rocky headlands (the tops of them a springy turf under one's feet) establishes itself at this far-westerly tip and continues all along the south coast of Llŷn. The long sweep known as Porth Neigwl (but in English, Hell's Mouth, into which a strong and heavy surf often rolls) is perhaps the best example of these spacious beaches, stretching as it does all the way to the peninsula's other extremity. If Braich y Pwll is the equivalent of Land's End, then Mynydd Cilan is the Lizard. And to continue this analogy, the area is also slightly less distinguished scenically.

Most people come to Abersoch from the other side. It is not only difficult, but rather perverse, to cross this headland from Porth Neigwl and come down into the village from behind. Most people, historically and today, come to it from the Pwllheli side. And it hardly seems an exaggeration to use the phrase in both its senses, because I have the firm impression that most people, at some time or other in their lives, have been to Abersoch.

Possibly to the rich young Midlanders who constitute so large a part of the present-day invasion, it would seem unlikely that the place had not been discovered suddenly by their generation, made accessible by the advent of the car, and made desirable by the universal ownership of sailing dinghies and speed-boats. So modern and smart is it now that they would find it hard to realize that it has been, for all its persisting old-Welsh-village façade, modern and smart for generations, and began to be so when their grandparents, for their part, were rich and young.

To the real discoverers of Abersoch 'before the war' means 1912. You should have seen it before the war. The overdressed and fading figures in the albums inhabit an empty beach, down to which they come each day with their hampers and rugs from the cottage which they have adventurously hired for the two months of the summer.

How they found it is a mystery. Why they thought it worthwhile to make the journey by train to Pwllheli and then by bus (getting off to enable it to climb Llanbedrog Hill) into this lonely, off-the-map place.

It was an adventure worthy, perhaps, of the time; and belonging to those who also turn up in more distant places, posing beside familiar monuments, but always wearing their stiff-collars and boaters, their big hats and stays and long dresses. You sent the servants on ahead, to the Abersoch cottage, with the trunks. A hamper regularly arrived from home during the summer, with edible goods which no one would expect to find in distant Wales. Cousins and their friends came to stay. It is strange to find that in this same place, where the first car-owners proudly paraded their enormous machines, the descendants and equivalents of these people now flock with their MGBs and their Lotuses. There is one overwhelming factor which distinguishes this new Abersoch generation from the last and the one before that. They are, like so many other categories of people, drastically more numerous.

Part of the secret of the place is the climate. Sunshine beats down for endless sandy summer afternoons, beating on the roofs of the beach-huts stacked against the slope, on the green but crowded south Caernarfon sea, on the hot sand lined with drawn-up yachts, on the brown and busy people. It is an imitation Côte d'Azur, but without the French and their inconvenient language; St Tropez-in-Llŷn. Part of its secret also is the anchorage, a safe and almost wind-proof bay which has become one of the largest small-boat centres in the country. Part of it of course is tradition. They go where their friends go, to have the security of being amongst others of the same type.

Wales is unpredictable, and Abersoch is one of its surprises. One would never expect to find these large businessmen in shorts parking their Bentleys in these lanes, or climbing the steps from the jetty to the yacht-club towards a gin-and-tonic overlooking the thirst-making sea, at the end of a long Welsh afternoon, and the purr of sports cars and speedboats, the sweep and splash of skis. It is part of a confident and expansive order of things which is, to put it mildly, incongruous in stony, chapel-going Llŷn.

Michael Senior: Portrait of North Wales (1973)

Abersoch

There was that headland, asleep on the sea,
The air full of thunder and the far air
Brittle with lightning; there was that girl
Riding her cycle, hair at half-mast,
And the men smoking, the dinghies at rest
On the calm tide. There were people going
About their business, while the storm grew
Louder and nearer and did not break.

Why do I remember these few things,
That were rumours of life, not life itself
That was being lived fiercely, where the storm raged?
Was it just that the girl smiled,
Though not at me, and the men smoking
Had the look of those who have come safely home?

R. S. Thomas (1913-2000)

Abererch

The village of Abererch, lush and leafy, with its low-browed, bright-washed cottages, gay with flowery frontages, straggles along the roadside to where the sparkling Erch rushes towards its tiny estuary. The old church might well tempt you to ask where the sexton lived and call for the keys. It is worth while only if you care for local history as written on church walls and in churchyards. There are beautiful glimpses, through screens of oak leaves, of the sea, brilliant in the blue of a sunny afternoon in the full height of summer. Pastures and meadows, green as in the west of Ireland, glow between hedges laden with honeysuckle and wild roses, while white farm-houses glint through the woods and grey roofs peer above the trees. The country hereabouts is no hillier than Warwickshire, but crystal streams sing with the voice of the mountain in the hollows; and old mill wheels drone on in half-hearted fashion as if conscious that their day was all but passed. Here, too, is an ancient barn, covered with ivy or virginia creeper, standing inconsequently in the fields; there a stone wall by the roadside, a rare study in tints, and bursting out in every fissure with the bloom of heather, foxglove, gorse, and lichen and a host of humble flowers whose names do not rip so readily to the tongue. There is nothing conventional in Welsh landscape; even where the land is flat it is rarely tame. Every hundred yards brings some fresh delight of foreground, with the great mountains hanging ever and always in the sky.

A. G. Bradley (1855-1945):
Highways and Byways of North Wales

Nant Gwrtheyrn

Before the bolted breakfast and the rush
To reach the yet unmissionaried depths of home
We had decided, with that instant faith
Which small boys use for certainty, it was a cave.
Stone cliffs as high as sight surrounded us
Along three sides encasing tracts in whose enormity
There surely lodged at least one wizard, several kings
And umpteen elves all reasonably tame.
Sometimes we joined them, feasting on such splendid fare
As boys prepare in the busy kitchens of the mind.

On days of doubt, which always came with cloud,
It could have been some gaping beast which gobbled us,
Though not on purpose, since deep inside his fat, primeval
                                                        belly
The flesh was sweet and green and smelled of celandines.
And out beyond the flinty jaws he had a mouth of seaside
Stuffed with sand and starfish and such rare snips
As kinder oceans bring for boys on beaches.
Some days the seas brought only stones but none as precious
As the one so big, we hoped, would seal our cave
In final insulation of our faith; it never came.

Much later over milk in classroom without benefit of biscuits
We had deduced our stony confines were a school.
The rock was hard. The school was made from rock, and hard.
So was the teacher sometimes, hard as flint.
Especially on Mondays. Secret drinker we were told.
Made his own. And needed to be secret
To drink on Sundays. Regretted Mondays.
But other times he spoke in wondrous recipes which made
Us almost taste the stone, sensing a hint of kin
As though it were some cast, ancestral spawn
Which gave us birth and life and even decoration in our death.

'Stone is a gift from God,' he'd say and turn
To Geography which was all gorse and grit
To which we listened, never quite believed
And knew he never quite expected it.

Was it at lunch when we first felt the stone
Was something which my father called security?
Not just the dumplings, solid though they were
Nor Mam, all aproned and available,
Or Grandad's cough, each quarter hour, like chimes,
Or grace on Sundays when the roast arrived.
It was that through each window of the house
The rock wrapped round us like an overcoat
Buttoned with boulders, pine sewn with heather-hem
Cocooning us from cold and heathen gusts
And winds and storms which other people had.
Inside our private stone, hewn from the mother rock,
We wintered, doubly wrapped and warm.

Or was it in chapel on stiff suited Sundays
When answers came to those confused in pew?
Not preacher's words, which offered nourishment of sorts,
But words of prayer, which seem to rise above the stone
Beyond the buzzards, birds of prey.
And louder still the singing till the air
Hung thick with hymn ascending and crescending
Through one great vital chancel whose walls were tall
And true and carved for choirs; in one almighty mixing bowl
Of glorying to God and man and stone and song
All undivided, indivisible, to men whose flesh appeared
To fall from them in dust on doorsteps before tea
And yet who found a kind of worship in their work.
Our fathers, which ate their heaven
Who gorged the stone and spewed it out on strangers' soil
In little geometric heaps for people to have babies in.
For stone was barter for our bread and bread was stone

And home was stone and familied with children
Quarried from the basalt of their faith
Preserved and sealed with everlasting contract.

It was at supper when they said the stone had died
From something which they felt was lack of need.
No call for it, they said, although the men
Had always listened when there was, responding as they did
More from tradition than tomorrow's custom.
God, in my wisdom, though not his, I thought
Had now removed and found another house
Made out of brick and plastic slate which never knew
The dust of men, somewhere beyond Caernarvon.
And we were moving too, like stone age men
Released from darkness into deeper dark,
Which comes from fear of finding more than loss.

On the beach with furniture and birds in cages
Waiting to be funnelled into lurching boats
I looked back once more at my village rock.
The walls were tall and towered still
But were they greyer, colder than before?
And were the chilly summits curving in?

As though to reunite in roof, enclosing emptiness?
There was no doubting now. It was a tomb,
A silent, songless, fresh vacated sepulchre.
Down in the tide the slowly shoving sea
Still pushed its pebbled debris to the sand
But not the final stone. We knew that would not come.
There was no call for it. The Occupant had gone.
Leaving three lines of print inside a glossy guide
For tourists who descend on Sundays with their sandwiches
And go home hungry

Geoffrey Newson

In 1960 the last family left Nant Gwrtheyrn and it fell into a ruinous state. It is now a Welsh national icon, the home of the Welsh Language Learning Centre.

A Visit to Carn Bodvean

In the final decade of the nineteenth century the novelist George Gissing spent some time on Llŷn.
When he came to write The Whirlpool *he set a part of the work on the peninsula.*

... a shapeless cairn rose above tree-tops, bare to the dazzling sky. As they issued from the shelter of the wood, a breeze buffeted about them, but only for a moment; then the air grew still, and nothing was audible but a soft whispering among the boughs below. The larches circling this stony height could not grow to their full stature; beaten, riven, stunted, by fierce blasts from mountain or from wave, their trunks were laden, and their branches thickly matted, with lichen so long and hoary that it gave them an aspect of age incalculable. Harvey always looked upon them with reverence, if not with awe.

In the sunny stillness their eyes wandered far and wide, around a vast horizon. On two sides lay the sea; to the west, bounded only where it met the blue sky above (though yonder line of cloud might perchance be the hills of Wicklow); eastward, enfolded by the shores of a great bay, with mountains on the far side, faintly visible through silvery vapour. Northward rose a noble peak, dark, stern, beautiful in the swift fall of curving rampart to the waves that broke at its foot; loftier by the proximity of two summits, sharp-soaring like itself, but unable to vie with it. Alone among the nearer mountains, this crest was veiled; smitten by sea-gusts, it caught and held them, and churned them into sunny cloudlets, which floated away in long fleecy rank, far athwart the clear depths of sky. Farther inland, where the haze of the warm morning hung and wavered, loomed at moments some grander form, to be imagined rather than descried; a glimpse of heights which, as the day wore on, would slowly reveal themselves and bask in the broad glow under crowning Snowdon.

'We have time! We can stay here!' said Mrs Abbott, moved with a profound delight.

'We have an hour at least. The sun is too hot; you must sit on the shadowed side of the cairn.'

The great silence had nothing of that awesomeness which broods in the mountain calm of wilder solitudes. Upon their ear fell the long low hush of the wood, broken suddenly from time to time by a fitful wind, which flapped with hollow note around the great heap of stones, whirled as if in sport, and was gone. Below, in leafy hollows, sounded the cry of a jay, the laugh of a woodpecker; from far heath and meadow trembled the bleat of lambs. Nowhere could be discovered a human form; but man's dwellings, and the results of his labour, painted the wide landscape in every direction. On mountain sides, and across the undulating lowland, wall or hedge mapped his conquests of nature, little plots won by the toil of successive generations for pasture or for tillage, won from the reluctant wilderness, which loves its fern and gorse, its mosses and heather. Near and far were scattered the little white cottages, each a gleaming speck, lonely, humble; set by the side of some long-winding, unfrequented road, or high on the green upland, trackless save for the feet of those who dwelt there.

George Gissing (1857-1903): The Whirlpool

Aberdaron

When I am old and honoured,
  With silver in my purse,
All criticism over,
  All men singing my praise,
I will purchase a lonely cottage
  With nothing facing its door
But the cliffs of Aberdaron
  And the wild waves on the shore.

When I am old and honoured,
  And my blood is running chill,
And watching the moon rising
  Stirs in my heart no thrill,
Hope will be mine thereafter
  In a cottage with its door
To the cliffs of Aberdaron
  And the wild waves on the shore.

When I am old and honoured
  Beyond all scorn and acclaim,
And my song goes by the rubric
  And gone is its passion's flame,
Hope will be mine thereafter
  In a cottage with its door
To the cliffs of Aberdaron
  And the wild waves on the shore.

For there I will discover
  In the stormy wind and its cry
Echoes of the old rebellion
  My soul knew in days gone by.
And I will sing with the old passion
  While gazing through the door
At the cliffs of Aberdaron
  And the wild waves on the shore.

Robert Evans Jones (Cynan) (1895-1970)
(translated by Joseph P. Clancy)

Hell's Mouth

I never saw a place which presented so favourable an appearance, and that was at the same time so much dreaded by the mariners, as the present. It is at the very end of the promontory, and from point to point is supposed to measure about eight miles: it is also nearly semicircular. None but strange vessels, even in the most boisterous weather, ever seek for shelter here, and when these are so unfortunate, they are soon stranded, and never again return. 'We remember (says Mr Jones, in one of his letters) more misfortunes to have happened in this bay, and more inhumanity shewn to the sufferers, than we have ever heard of any where else on the Welsh coast.' My pilot, who had been long acquainted with every part of these coasts, informed me, that, from whatever point of the compass the wind blew, out at sea, on account of the surrounding high rocks, it always came into the mouth of this bay; and from whatever quarter the tide flowed, the upper current here always sets inwards! From these circumstances the common tradition is, that the place obtained the appellation of *Hell's Mouth*.

William Bingley (1774-1823): North Wales,
delineated from two excursions

Traverse Above the Sea
November, 1984

There are no better situated mountains south of the Scottish border than the trio called Yr Eifl, half hanging above Bae Caernarfon with conical summits draped across the sky of Llŷn. Seen from the sandy lands of Newborough or Malltraeth's mouth they rear from the water like giants, the highest land of the peninsula they surely dominate.

The other day we walked the seaside pastures where Welsh Mountain ewes seemed rugged-up against the autumn chill, chewing cud as they gazed to the blue-grey horizon where no ship sailed. The northernmost hill reaches only 1,458 feet but presents a granite face reminiscent of the Drum's west side. To traverse between it and the waves necessitates an airy passage several hundred feet above vertical cliffs and as we made for this, along the boulder beach, a silver shape ahead turned out to be an Atlantic grey seal pup. It was but a few days old and moaned and pursed its lips at us. Its mother eyed us from the rolling sea so we left it on the lonely perch where thrift blooms in June, crooning an innocent farewell by the empty shore.

Beyond the rocky point of Trwyn-y-gorlech comes easier ground where stands one of Wales's most isolated settlements. Porth-y-Nant was a quarry village looking out over a bay where once granite was loaded onto boats; when the quarries closed the inhabitants left until only a coastguard and his sister remained. In 1964 they departed and Porth-y-Nant steadily decayed, over-run with bracken and rent by westerly gales. Now it is being restored by students of the Welsh language.

As we went up onto the seaward flank of Yr Eifl the view broadened again and on the descent to Trefor the white tower of Ynys Llanddwyn's defunct lighthouse flashed in the afternoon sunshine a dozen miles to the north. The great red bulk of Yr Eifl's empty quarry building reared beside us, a rusting Potala high above the Welsh sea.

Roger Redfern: A Snowdonia Country Diary (2004)

Tŷ Newydd is the national writers' centre for Wales and is situated at Llanystumdwy. It was the final home of David Lloyd George, who spent his youth in the area. Steve Griffiths has tutored poetry-writing courses at Tŷ Newydd.

Tŷ Newydd

A supple, determined V of geese
follows the line of the surf,
knowing September into the stiff wind:
flecks of whitecaps above them
reach to the indistinct
hinge of the sky.

I listened for that hinge:
my whisper came back to me
like the surf across the railway line
and up the hill, but it was busy, busy,
building hypotheses,
stakes for the heart.

The memory of power
brushed me, and I thought
of the day I first dressed myself
and I stood up
and surveyed the distance to the floor
that pushed up towards me.

Then the paradox of generosity
called by
in a daydream of a place
where people lock the door
and leave the key on the outside
in welcome to the unexpected guest –

or – with the stillness at my back
as I turn away from the empty room –

locking the inside in.
So I climbed away:
there was a delicious cold sweat
under my shirt for the wind to play on.

There were green shoots among burned heather
in dense cloud, and I heard wings:
they were the flutter of brown paper
unwrapped in another room:
they were the poetry shut in
with misgivings, a concealed offer.

Steve Griffiths

A Vivid Experience

. . . we turned west into the attractive wooded countryside of
the Lleyn peninsula; alas, that obstinate haze continued to
deny us the marine views in their perfection. We stopped to
visit the Lloyd George Museum which houses the trophies of
his resplendent career. Llanystumdwy is delightful, a bower
of blue hydrangeas, full in the sun's eye. We then entered a
countryside of agreeable remoteness to reach, ten miles
farther on, Plas-yn-Rhiw, a small seventeenth-century manor
house buried in the trees of Mynydd Rhiw. Here live the
three Misses Keating who have already given part of the fifty
acres round the house to the Trust and bequeathed to it the
house and the rest. They have also this very year (1950) given
fifty acres of cliffland on Mynydd Cilan with a wonderful
view of Cardigan Bay.

Our hostesses insisted on keeping us for a delicious
lunch, and we spent a completely delightful couple of hours
at Plas-yn-Rhiw. The only thing that refused to play its part
was the view which sulked in the haze. It was in vain for me
to vow that I could imagine what a vision of sea and
mountains would be revealed upon the right day; I was

assured that, however beautiful I might fancy it, the beauty of it in reality would exceed my liveliest fancy. It would have mattered less if a sea-fog had descended to annihilate the view altogether. What the Misses Keating lamented was the way that the view was still there, all its distant outlines blurred by haze and all its colour drained to an indeterminate and dreary grey. But Plas-yn-Rhiw will always remain for me a vivid experience in spite of that mischievous haze, and if I did not see the view I did see a great mauve *Iris Kaempferi* all by itself beside a grey wall which seemed to me the most beautiful iris I had ever seen.

Compton Mackenzie (1883-1972): I Took A Journey

Penllyn

Sun's slap on a white wall,
burnt shadows in fields

wrens shade their small hearts.

All night I thought of Enlli,
her faint breathing

an island asleep
under a bedspread of green.

Oyster-catchers pipe
their stone-bag throats.

Paths hot-wire around us,
my forehead sings with sweat.

Gwyn Parry

Nant Gwrtheyrn

Clouds accumulate, darkening
The worn face of the mountain. The striped
Cry of the oyster-catcher cuts
The sky. Impossible to join the spaces.

One mass against another. Frail
Sounds falling like ribbons or wounds.
Bits creeping, vegetation,
Distraction under the small rain.

The sisters clump up the Nant in boots,
Damp hair close to the forehead, sorrel
In warm folds of the palm, feathers
And granite sugar, so far ahead.

One lingers on the path, smooth grass
Where sheep have nibbled. The blue husk
Of a tiger beetle cradled there
Is spiritless, an Egyptian relic.

It is borne up the valley, joining
One thing with another. The day
Lightens. Clouds break up the sky.
Jerseys are tied around the waist.

The spaces grow between them, dislinked
On the gradient, frowning and looking
Back. The battered sky opens.
The treasures slip from opening fingers.

John Fuller

Walking below Carn Guwch

It's going fast. Old roads
Are green again and gates
Tied up. The little church
Shares its field with a blind
Congregation of straggling
Mushrooms. Below, the river
Bends as we expect it
To, attended by curlews
That no map needs to show.

It's going fast and we
Will never find it once
It's gone. Not in stone
Or surprising photographs,
Not in handwriting
Or careful recipes.
Far from our sealed diseases
We sense it in the river
And the sadness of the curlews.

It's going fast. Somehow
It rises on the wind,
A metamorphosis
Of an idea pursued
Until it took quick fright.
The bodies of the children
Are budding, an old response
Which says: It's our world now
And going on forever.

John Fuller

People

Young Fellow From Llŷn

Young fellow from Llŷn, who's the girl of your heart,
You who wander so late in the evening apart?
My sweetheart is young and she comes from the Sarn,
And neat is her cottage that's under the Garn.

And what does she look like, the girl of your heart,
You who wander so late in the evening apart?
Dark, dark is my darling and dark haired is she,
But white shines her body like foam on the sea.

And what is she wearing, the girl of your heart,
You who wander so late in the evening apart?
In a long gown of shining white satin she goes
And red in her bosom there blushes a rose.

Young fellow from Llŷn, is she angry and flown,
That you wander so late in the evening alone?
Oh, never my sweetheart showed anger or pride
Since the very first time that we walked side by side.

Young fellow from Llŷn, why do tears then start
To your eyes as you wander so late and apart?
From her cheek Death has withered the roses away
And white is the wear in the cottage of clay.

William Jones (1896-1961)
(translated by Harri Webb)

Welsh Incident

'But that was nothing to what things came out
From the sea-caves of Criccieth yonder.'
'What were they? Mermaids? dragons? ghosts?'
'Nothing at all of any things like that.'
'What were they, then?'
                              'All sorts of queer things,
Things never seen or heard or written about,
Very strange, un-Welsh, utterly peculiar
Things. Oh, solid enough they seemed to touch,
Had anyone dared it. Marvellous creation,
All various shapes and sizes, and no sizes,
All new each perfectly unlike his neighbour,
Though all came moving slowly out together.'
'Describe just one of them.
                              'I am unable.'
'What were their colours?'
                              'Mostly nameless colours,
Colours you'd like to see; but one was puce
Or perhaps more like crimson, but not purplish.
Some had no colour.'
                              'Tell me, had they legs?'
'Not a leg nor foot among them that I saw.'
'But did these things come out in any order?
What o'clock was it? What was the day of the week?
Who else was present? How was the weather?'
'I was coming to that, It was half-past three
On Easter Tuesday last. The sun was shining.
The Harlech Silver Band played *Marchog Iesu*
On thirty-seven shimmering instruments,
Collecting for Caernarvon's (Fever) Hospital Fund.
The populations of Pwllheli, Criccieth,
Portmadoc, Borth, Tremadoc, Penrhyndeudraeth
Were all assembled. Criccieth's mayor addressed them
First in good Welsh and then in fluent English,
Twisting his fingers in his chain of office,

Welcoming the things. They came out on the sand,
Not keeping time to the band, moving seaward
Silently at a snail's pace. But at last
The most odd, indescribable thing of all,
Which hardly one man there could see for wonder,
Did something recognizably a something.'
'Well, what?'
                           'It made a noise.'
                                          'A frightening noise?'
'No, no.
                 'A musical noise? A noise of scuffling?'
'No, but a very loud, respectable noise –
Like groaning to oneself on Sunday morning
In Chapel, close before the second psalm.'
'What did the mayor do?'
                           'I was coming to that.'

Robert Graves (1895-1985)

The Tylwyth Teg

There were, says the story, at a small harbour belonging to
Nefyn, some houses in which several families formerly lived;
the houses are there still, but nobody lives in them now.
There was one family there to which a little girl belonged;
they used to lose her for hours every day; so her mother was
very angry with her for being so much away. 'I must know,'
said she, 'where you go for your play.' The girl answered that
it was to Pin-y-Wig, 'The Wig Point,' which means a place to
the west of the Nefyn headland; it was there, she said, she
played with many children. 'They are very nice children –
much nicer,' said the child, 'than I am.' 'I must know whose
children they are,' was the reply; and one day the mother
went with her little girl to see the children. It was a distance
of about a quarter of a mile to Pin-y-Wig, and after climbing
the slope and walking a little along the top they came in sight

of the Pin. It is from this Pin that the people of Pen-yr-Allt get water, and it is from there they get it still. Now after coming near the Pin the little girl raised her hands with joy at the sight of the children. 'Oh, mother,' said she, 'their father is with them to-day; he is not with them always; it is only sometimes that he is.' The mother asked the child where she saw them. 'There they are, mother, running down to the Pin, with their father sitting down.' 'I see nobody, my child,' was the reply, and great fear came upon the mother; she took hold of the child's hand in terror, and it came to her mind at once that they were the *Tylwyth Teg*. Never afterwards was the little girl allowed to go to Pin-y-Wig: the mother had heard that the Tylwyth Teg exchanged people's children with their own.

Edward Thomas (1878-1917): Beautiful Wales

The Farmers of Llŷn

Nowhere, even in Wales, are there thriftier, harder working and more independent farmers than those of Lleyn. The women milk the cows, make the butter, and look after the marketing of lesser products, and work in the fields in hay and even harvest time. The men do all the outdoor work, only hiring labour, which as elsewhere in Wales is scarce and dear, when absolutely compelled to. Farmhouse fare is of a notoriously Spartan kind all over North Wales, and nowhere more so than here. Fresh meat is rarely tasted. Here, as elsewhere, it is customary to kill the least marketable beast upon the place, a dry cow or a venerable bull, and put it into brine for the year's supply of meat. Pieces are then cut off it from time to time by the careful housewife, and used to strengthen or subsidise the staple dishes of the table. In nine farmhouses out of ten in Caernarvonshire the menu will be much as follows. For breakfast, barley bread and buttermilk; for dinner, potatoes and buttermilk, with a piece of salt meat from the brine pot; for tea, bread with butter or cheese, while porridge and buttermilk are served for supper when the day's work is ended.

S. Baring Gould (1853-1927): A Book of North Wales

Ranks and Degrees

Life as the parson's son in such a place and at such a time was not therefore the structured, middle-class existence of literary vicarages and sons of clergy. It was both separate and entirely involved. Separate in the physical reality of large houses; involved because of the ancient organic unity of society in Llŷn in those days. To describe it as classless would be to use the term anachronistically. There were ranks and degrees, people had their functions and they walked the paths ordained by providence. There was a stability and predictability about people's social movements that had by-passed the Industrial Revolution; the pattern of events, both for the community and the individual, was entirely dictated by the natural cycle. Apart from the largely undeveloped tourist trade, the whole locality was geared to agriculture. Those who were not farmers serviced the farming community, either as shopkeepers or teachers or ministers of religion. Social events were subservient to the needs of ploughing, sowing and harvesting; little or nothing was organized during the summer months; concerts, dramatic performances, whist drives, eisteddfodau. All took place during the long dark winter evenings, all the darker during my childhood for the imposition of the blackout. I hovered around such events, watching the adults and carrying kettles and flower vases. As I grew older, all such social gatherings during the hours of darkness provided exciting, stolen moments with elusive and beautiful girls, tossing their dark hair in the wind that always howled around village halls in Llŷn on winter nights. That constant south-westerly often carried driving rain as well, but we happily huddled in the lee of corrugated-iron porticos and under the slanting lights from the hall windows. Inside would be warm and organized, choirs singing, adults in overcoats playing cards, but outside in the cold dark we would tease out each other's responses, touch, slap and tickle in a breathless excitement and laugh uncertainly at each other's responses, until some wondering adult would thrust a censorious head through the door and put an end to our socializing. Everything that happened, happened annually, regularly, and was part of an unchanging, totally predictable cycle of events.

Human considerations and human decisions really counted for very little. Some people were no doubt regarded as being of a superior social order, but I knew no one outside the squirearchy who was rich. Rich people, people who owned luxury goods and kept servants, people who drove a great deal in polished cars lived, if at all, in Abersoch and not in the heart of Llŷn.

R. Gerallt Jones (1934-1999): A Place in the Mind

A Funeral in Llŷn

From the Garn's summit
a pattern is visible.

Small fields, gorse hedgerows,
a tidy topographic quilt,
and the ffridd of bilberry and fern
assenting, if reluctantly,
in the conspiracy.

And so with our society.
Every relationship was patterned,
the fruit of interwoven years
of careful pruning and hedging and closing gaps,

of knowing the nature of each gateway,
of knowing, as the need arose,
when to lock the gates.

Then death came,
the volcano of human topography.
We can only watch the lava flowing,
its primitive shapelessness penetrating,
civilised hedgerows laid waste,
everything sharp-cornered,
today as it was at the beginning,
before order was established.

It is now that we stand naked
staring wildly at each other;
no gates to close,
one man's land in another man's field,
so uncompromising the indiscriminate sea
that flooded in.

Tomorrow, the hedges will be rebuilt,
the gaps closed,
and the day after a new safe
pattern;
we shall again walk seemly through the appropriate
                                                        gateway,
but today a volcano erupted
and we stare
            into each other's eyes
naked.

R. Gerallt Jones (1934-1999)
(translated by the poet)

Ffynnon Fair

(Joan Abbott Parry was drowned in the sea at Ffynnon Fair in July 1904, shortly before her sixteenth birthday. Her younger brother saw her fall, and broke the news first to their father: 'Father, I must whisper this . . . ')

The men saw the sway of blue serge dress caught
On rocks by Ffynnon Fair, and lifted her above the swell,
Climbed the rough steps with the tide's burden between
Them, the unutterable. How she must have, as she fell,
caught her breath, clutched at startled air, before blue-green
Surge of sea clutched and kept her gasp.

Her father drew a line and shadow on sunlit page,
Defined the shape of Ynys Enlli, their pilgrimage.
Father, I must whisper this, her brother said
My sister has fallen.

Now the women of the parish lay her out
And wash her. Their hands only are able to define
Her high cheek-bone, young breast, they know like lovers
The thin-ridged beauty of her spine.
They tease the flecks of seaweed from her hair.

I must whisper this.

Each year her mother turned the legend of the well:
*A woman's unutterable wish fulfilled by water
Carried from the perfect shape of Ffynnon Fair
Unspilt, up to the clifftop church.* Her daughter
In this, her fifteenth year, took down a cup.

Father, I must whisper this.

Perhaps she broke the water's surface first, and spoke her wish.
The women of the parish know her prayer.

Her mother understood her faith.
With the salt taste caught in her own breath,
She whispers all of it to be undone,
To see her daughter climb the broken steps again,
Holding whole her own life, like unspilt water.

Michael Ponsford

Dick Aberdaron

Richard Jones of Aberdaron was surely the most prodigious intellectual freak that ever came out of Wales . . . He had certainly the gift of tongues, and a mania for acquiring them under discouraging circumstances, developed to a degree that gives him a place to himself among village prodigies. He was the son of an illiterate carpenter, and the descendant of generations of rude Lleyn peasants. It is more than likely none of his ancestors could even read or write. But Dick himself died at sixty, the master, more or less, of thirty-five languages, as it is said. Let us for safety's sake reduce the number by one-half, and at the same time remark that he also died as he had lived, a frowsy, dirty peasant, or worse than a peasant: a loafer rather and a stroller, filthy in person, part mendicant part medicine man: one quarter idiot, three quarters genius: the owner of an abnormal brain, if ever there was one. But where did the craving for strange tongues and the capacity for acquiring them come from? The query might well give a physiologist some food for serious contemplation.

Dick fell foul of his parents, or they rather of him, at a tender age. He had no schooling, but hung about the village schoolroom, and by the help of books he found lying about there, and of good-natured boys who had mastered the art, he learned to read in Welsh. Soon afterwards, by the same laborious methods, he acquired English. At twenty he was still a hopeless failure at his father's trade, till, tired of being cursed and beaten, he left Lleyn, and wandered to Bangor and thence to Liverpool. When he came across an Italian or a German pedlar it was his habit to stick to him till he had learned enough of his language to form a basis for future study. It was not, however, the art of conversation in foreign tongues, dead or living, that Dick so much sought after, though even in this he appears to have been glib enough, but grammars and dictionaries were his especial joy. Hebrew he learned from tattered books that chance threw in his way. Latin and Greek he mastered with equal facility and by the same means. French, Russian, Scandinavian, all came in course of time to this road-side, tramp scholar. Patrons in plenty such a man found: bishops, clergymen, and tradesmen. They gave him work in their gardens or stables which he never did, and lent him grammars and dictionaries over which he pored with pen, ink, and paper. He was too filthy in person for the inside of a decent house, and so bizarre in appearance that he was the butt of street boys through his whole long life. He would neither work nor wash. There are plenty of pictures of him extant which show a face and head covered with bushy black hair, from which peered two bright beady eyes. His dress was rugged and uncouth, and he carried his precious library concealed about his person, which gave the latter an inflated and abnormal appearance. The way in which he clung to his books in periods of penury and semi-starvation gives much pathos to a narrative that is otherwise uncanny and unnatural. He had no ambition, except to acquire fresh languages, no thought for the morrow, no regard for money, scarcely any even for food. At one time he developed a tendency for more pronounced posing, adopting a cast-off blue and silver cavalry jacket as a dress and a cap of hare's skin with the ears sticking up as a head-gear. From the ears hung pieces of cloth, on which were inscribed sentences in Greek and Hebrew, and thus attired he would drone out the song of Moses in Hebrew to astonished audiences in Welsh village streets. He carried a ram's horn too, slung round him, and blew upon it lusty blasts at the most inappropriate times.

Dick was a famous character throughout all North Wales, and he wandered once as far as Dover, and was for some time in London. He never begged, nor drank. Hunger compelled him occasionally to work, but he seemed to think that the public ought to supply his simple wants, and indeed they did so, after a fashion. His linguistic accomplishments were useless for any practical purpose. It was the construction of language – its roots and grammar that fascinated him. Nor had he the least desire for the information conveyed in their literature. He was a thorough philologist and scholar of the old school was Dick in this respect, but his facility was as great as his ardour. A learned don from Oxford who once sought an interview with him in Wales put him on to construe Homer, carefully keeping the breadth of the table between himself and the frowsy bundle of rags that represented the poor student. Dick, however, proved himself quite equal to the doctor's tests, but with the unconscious enthusiasm of a scholar and a purist waxed contemptuously indignant when his reverend examiner began to question him regarding the personality of the heroes in the Iliad and touched upon the story therein contained. Had any one been found to wash and dress Dick of Aberdaron, and send him to the University, there is no doubt that it is to the Cambridge of his day that he should have gone! Though Dick was first and chiefly, according to his rude lights, a scholar, contemporary authorities entitled to credence declare that he could speak fourteen languages fluently. He would never ask charity, though he both expected and accepted it, and had been reduced for some years before his death to telling fortunes. He was buried in St Asaph churchyard.

A. G. Bradley (1855-1945):
Highways and Byways of North Wales

Melancholy Pleasure

Samuel Johnson visited North Wales in 1774 in the company of his close friend Hesta Thrale. Their excursions took them to Llŷn and a visit was made to Mrs Thrale's birthplace.

August 22. We went to visit Bodville, the place where Mrs Thrale was born; and the Churches called Tydweiliog and Llangwinodyl, which she holds by impropriation.

We had an invitation to the house of Mr Griffiths of Bryn y dol, where we found a small neat new built house, with square rooms: the walls are of unhewn stone, and therefore thick; for the stones not fitting with exactness, are not strong without great thickness. He had planted a great deal of young wood in walks.

August 24. We went to see Bodville. Mrs Thrale remembered the rooms, and wandered over them with recollection of her childhood. This species of pleasure is always melancholy. The walk was cut down, and the pond was dry. Nothing was better.

We surveyed the Churches, which are mean, and neglected to a degree scarcely imaginable. They have no pavement, and the earth is full of holes. The seats are rude benches; the Altars have no rails. One of them has a breach in the roof. On the desk, I think, of each lay a folio Welsh Bible of the black letter, which the curate cannot easily read. Mr Thrale purposes to beautify the Churches, and if he prospers, will probably restore the tithes. The two parishes are, Llangwinodyl and Tydweiliog. The Methodists are here very prevalent. A better church will impress the people with more reverence of public worship.

Mrs Thrale visited a house where she had been used to drink milk, which was left, with an estate of two hundred pounds a year, by one Lloyd, to a married woman who lived with him.

We went to Pwllheli, a mean old town, at the extremity of the country.

Samuel Johnson (1709-1784): Journal of a Journey into Wales

Gracious Courtesy and Charity

In his youth Thomas de Quincey's wanderings on foot around North Wales eventually brought him to Llanystumdwy. He describes the outcome of this visit in Confessions of an English Opium Eater.

. . . I was entertained for upwards of three days by a family of young people, with an affectionate and fraternal kindness that left an impression upon my heart not yet impaired. The family consisted, at that time, of four sisters and three brothers, all grown-up, and remarkable for elegance and delicacy of manners. So much beauty, or so much native good breeding and refinement, I do not remember to have seen before or since in any cottage, except once or twice in Westmoreland and Devonshire. They spoke English; an accomplishment not often met with in so many members of one Welsh family, especially in villages remote from the high road. Here I wrote, on my first introduction, a letter about prize-money for one of the brothers, who had served on board an English man-of-war; and, more privately, two letters to sweethearts for two of the sisters. They were both interesting in appearance; and one of uncommon loveliness. In the midst of their confusion and blushes, whilst dictating, or rather giving me general instructions, it did not require any great penetration to discover that they wished their letters to be as kind as was consistent with proper maidenly reserve. I contrived so to temper my expressions as to reconcile the gratification of both feelings; and they were as much pleased with the way in which I had given expression to their thoughts, as (in their simplicity) they were astonished at my having so readily discovered them. The reception one meets with from the women of a family generally determines the tenor of one's whole entertainment. In this case I had discharged my confidential duties as secretary so much to the general satisfaction, perhaps also amusing them with my conversation, that I was pressed to stay; and pressed with a cordiality which I had little inclination to resist. I slept unavoidably with the brothers, the only unoccupied bed standing in the chamber of the young women: but in all other points they treated me with a respect not usually paid to purses as light as mine; making it evident that my scholarship and courteous demeanour were considered sufficient arguments of gentle blood. Thus I lived with them for three days, and great part of a fourth; and, from the undiminished kindness which they continued to show me, I believe that I might have stayed with them up to this time, if their power had corresponded with their wishes. On the last morning, however, I perceived upon their countenances, as they sat at breakfast, the approach of some unpleasant communication; and soon after, one of the brothers explained to me that, on the day before my arrival, their parents had gone to an annual meeting of Methodists, held at Carnarvon, and in the course of that day were expected to return; 'and if they should not be so civil as they ought to be,' he begged, on the part of all the young people, that I would not take it amiss. The parents returned with churlish faces, and '*Dym Sassenach*' (*no English*) in answer to all my addresses. I saw how matters stood; and so, taking an affectionate leave of my kind and interesting young hosts, I went my way. For, though they spoke warmly to their parents on my behalf, and often excused the manner of the old people by saying that it was 'only their way', yet I easily understood that my talent for writing love-letters would do as little to recommend me with two sexagenarian Welsh Methodists as my Greek Sapphics or Alcaics; and what had been hospitality, when offered with the gracious courtesy of my young friends, would become charity, when connected with the harsh demeanour of their parents.

Thomas de Quincey (1774-1823):
Confessions of an English Opium Eater

Sir Howell y Fwyall

A native of the adjoining parish of Llanstyndwy, was constable of this castle. This valiant officer attended the Black Prince in the battle of Poitiers, where, although on foot, and armed only with a battle-axe, he performed several acts of the utmost bravery and heroism. The principal of his services was the cutting off the head of the French king's horse, and taking him prisoner. As a recompence for his valour he received the honour of knighthood, and was allowed to bear the arms of France, with a 'battle-axe in bend sinister'; and to add to his name y Fwyall, *the battle-axe*. In further commemoration of his services, it was ordered that a mess of meat should, at the expence of the crown, be every day served up before the axe with which he had performed these wonderful feats. This mess, after it had been brought to the knight, was taken down, and distributed among the poor. Even after Sir Howel's death the mess continued to be served as usual, and for the sake of his soul, given to the poor till so lately as the beginning of the reign of Queen Elizabeth. Eight yeomen attendants, called yeomen of the crown, were appointed to guard it, who received each eight-pence a day constant wages. The present parish clerk of Criccieth informed a gentleman of my acquaintance, that in digging a grave in the church-yard, about ten years ago, he found a human skull of enormous size, holding in the cavity for the brain more than two quarts of water. He used it for some time, in the place of a more convenient implement, to throw water out of newly opened graves; and supposed it to have been the skull of this renowned hero, probably, however, without any other reason, than from its enormous size: for the ignorant generally associate the idea of gigantic stature with the character of a valiant man.

*William Bingley(1774-1823): North Wales,
delineated from two excursions*

A Troublesome Butler

Between Abersoch and Llanbedrog on the Lleyn Peninsula there was a house called Castel March. In the seventeenth century it was the home of Sir William Jones, the local squire and Justice of the Peace, who was on excellent terms with a gang of smugglers who used to run their cargoes ashore under Llanbedrog head. The squire was a jovial, easy-going man who enjoyed simple pleasures like hunting the hare in the Llanbedrog hills and getting drunk with his cronies at Pwllheli market. The only fly in the warm amber of his days was a butler who bullied him abominably. Though he was sacked many times, the servant ignored the dismissals and continued to plague his master. In desperation the squire begged the skipper of the smugglers' sloop to kidnap the bullying butler. A price was agreed and some nights later the smugglers let themselves into Castell March, seized, bound and gagged the servant and dragged him off to ship him to some foreign coast and there abandon him. But the butler proved so amiable a companion, so inventive a criminal, that instead he was sworn in as a member of the gang. In the year that followed he took command.

The vessel was away for a year or two pursuing a successful career of piracy before it returned to Llanbedrog. This time it was the squire's turn to be bound, gagged and kidnapped. When morning broke, he lay trussed on the deck of the sloop watching the vanishing coast of Lleyn. This time the butler had power of life and death over him. Many years passed and a good deal of sea water under the prow before Sir William was exchanged for a heavy ransom. When he was freed, he removed instantly to Caernarfon, where he spent the remainder of his days in the shadow of the castle. And no doubt always looking over his shoulder in case the butler did it again.

Ian Skidmore: Gwynedd (1986)

The Vicar

. . . we left Pentrefelin and moved into a pleasant house on the Broomhall estate. It had the strange name of Doltrement, and stood on a gentle slope overlooking the sweep of Cardigan Bay and close to the village of Abererch. Protected from the south-west wind by a small church-topped hill, the stone-built houses faced each other across a road that meandered down to the old bridge over the Erch. Hydrangeas grew among the cobbles in front of the windows.

The vicar was the Rev. R. Wynne-Griffiths, a cheery little chestnut of a man who had been a convert from Nonconformism. He was in his seventies when we came there and found it hard to carry the whole burden of the service on his shoulders. I was asked to read the lessons, and this I did, on condition that I chose my own. I now feel that I must have been a dreadful hypocrite, but it certainly eased his Sunday labours. His sermons were always read from some tract sent to him weekly. He used to stand in the pulpit, his small red face barely visible over the top, and read to us like a schoolmaster.

'And you may escape damnation by a hair's breadth,' he read. 'Hairs and not hares, breadth and not breath, my friends,' he would explain, spelling out each word, and my father, who was very deaf at the time, turned to me and bellowed: 'Can't hear a word the old fool says!'

It was my mother who felt it her duty as the daughter of a parson to instruct him in the proper paths, laid down through ecclesiastical centuries. Often the old man swayed up the path to the front door, sat heavily in the drawing-room and when he had really settled down my mother would launch her attack.

'Vicar, why did you have a purple frontal on the altar on Sunday?' she snapped. 'You know quite well it should have been white.'

'Well, Mrs Williams – '

'It's no good making excuses, Vicar. See there is a white one on next Sunday. And have you called on the Pollecoffs yet?'

The Pollecoffs, an orthodox Jewish family, had settled in a farm on the hill.

'Well, no, Mrs Williams.'

'And why not? They are very good people and send their servants to church regularly.'

'Well, Mrs Williams, you know what I feel about the Jews.'

'And what may that be?'

An unusual look of ferocity crept into the pink face of the vicar as he counter-attacked.

'I will never forgive them for what they did to Jesus Christ.'

'Stuff and nonsense!' said my mother.

The vicar staggered away to lick his wounds, and a few days later my mother complained, 'Can't understand the clergy these days, they never call.'

Kyffin Williams (1918-2006): Across the Straits

Taid and Nain

We always referred to our paternal grandparents in the Welsh form of 'Taid' and 'Nain'. Nain was the gentlest of all the Kyffins. Like her mother-in-law, she had to suffer the continual absence of her husband, for Owen, like his father, was dedicated to saving lives. He had gone out as a boy in the old Cemlyn lifeboat, so he knew how to master the rough seas. He had suffered as the oarsmen suffered in those days, when on reaching shore the ice had to be broken away from the hands that held the oars.

Taid's first parish was Boduan in West Caernarvonshire. Boduan is in the middle of the Lleyn Peninsula, a parish of woodland and bog dominated by Garn Boduan, a rocky lump, wooded on one side and with a group of old British stone dwellings near the top. From there you can look north to Anglesey, east to the Snowdon range and south to Cardigan bay; while to the west the peninsula stretches like a hoary finger to Aberdaron, pointing seawards to the distant Wicklow Mountains.

The parish was well suited to my grandfather, for he could look after the Porthdinllaen lifeboat on the north coast and the Abersoch lifeboat on Cardigan Bay. And once in the middle of a sermon a man ran down the aisle to tell of a ship in distress off Nefyn. Taid followed him out to his waiting cob and cantered away into the night. Sometimes he would return to one lifeboat house only to be summoned to the other, for a parson at the helm meant a lot to the superstitious crews.

When he first came to Boduan in 1862, a great storm drove fourteen ships ashore at Porthdinllaen. The locals stood on the cliffs and watched and waited to make their gruesome pickings, as one by one the sailors were swept from the rigging and drowned in the boiling sea. Taid railed at them and cursed them, exhorting them to help him save the sailors. They, surly and listless, wished him in hell and continued their greedy watch. Two men only joined him and with their help he saved twenty-four lives.

One January night in 1870, after trying to launch the lifeboat for four weary hours, he eventually left the bay at Abersoch and rowed out into the gale and the darkness to the help of the *Kenilworth* of New York, hard aground on St Patrick's Causeway. This was a shallow bank off Llanbedr that was a constant danger to shipping off the Merioneth coast. The *Kenilworth*'s main mizzen masts had gone and only a part of the foremast was standing when the lifeboat reached her. The captain and thirteen of the crew were rescued, but three weeks later the captain died, it is said, of a broken heart.

Kyffin Williams (1918-2006): Across the Straits

History and Culture

Sunset Over Llŷn
(from Llandanwg)

The day assimilating to night
and the bloodstained gloom like Catraeth's field.

One day more,
and how many fewer
speak the language of Gwrtheyrn?

The words of romance are powerless
in the twilight of the black figures.

Night,
do not be gentle,
be terrifying, hag-ridden;
chill us
to the marrow of our fear.
Be Hell,
with your hounds scratching our doors.

Let the teeth of Yr Eifl still bite the darkness
and the waves of Porth Neigwl torment the silence.

Let there be sleeplessness in Nefyn
and disquiet in the woods of Cefnamlwch.

Let our fever seethe
in the bitterness of the last hours.

Parishes of Llŷn's heartland,
fear the darkness,
and disdain
the peace of an easy death.

Sion Aled (translated by Grahame Davies)

The Moon in Lleyn

The last quarter of the moon
of Jesus gives way
to the dark; the serpent
digests the egg. Here
on my knees in this stone
church, that is full only
of the silent congregation
of shadows and the sea's
sound, it is easy to believe
Yeats was right. Just as though
choirs had not sung, shells
have swallowed them; the tide laps
at the Bible; the bell fetches
no people to the brittle miracle
of the bread. The sand is waiting
for the running back of the grains
in the wall into its blond
glass. Religion is over, and
what will emerge from the body
of the new moon, no one
can say.

      But a voice sounds
in my ear: Why so fast,
mortal? These very seas
are baptised. The parish
has a saint's name time cannot
unfrock. In cities that
have outgrown their promise people
are becoming pilgrims
again, if not to this place,
then to the recreation of it
in their own spirits. You must remain
kneeling. Even as this moon
making its way through the earth's

cumbersome shadow, prayer, too,
has its phases.

R. S. Thomas (1913-2000)

The Moons of Llŷn

(for R. S. Thomas)

The moon in Llŷn is pregnant,
like a womb on the verge of emptying:
the last quarter is already
spent, and from the bruised womb
language is thrusting itself,
language that isn't language unmaking
the language that has been language to us,
language that has been language to Mynytho,
Llanengan, Llangian, Rhoshirwaun, and Sarn,
and shy villages like Cilan.
The moon in Llŷn is filled with obliteration.

At the zenith of the obliteration's moon you came to Llŷn
as priest in its distress:
through the moons of the ages the first quarter's
zenith already was spent;
neither did you see
its second quarter washing the beach
with monolingual waves.
Your moon is obliterating's moon;
the last quarter's posterity's ebb.

I'm long acquainted with the moons in Llŷn:
in the lingering third quarter
the moon was the moon of creation
in Pen Llŷn to a muddled child:
the Welsh moon above Porth Neigwl

scattering sparks like words
through the pages of the water;
Porth Ceiriad's moon like wax
rubbing yellow against the night,
putting a shine on the golden
beads of stars above Abersoch,
and Bardsey's moon a consecrated
host above the bay's purple altar.

It isn't easy by now
to return to Llŷn: the darkness of a downcast moon
signifies the dying of a lineage,
foretells the end of this land.
If I take a step upon it
in memory, it is Tir na n-Og,
but when I return, come summer, to Llŷn
I am Osian hearing the mournful
music of the language dying in the sea.
Where the language with its chime once graced
my contemporaries' lips,
I am the last wave that breaks
on the beach of our identity.

Your moon is not the moon of creation
but an egg on the brink of hatching
obliteration: the moon in Llŷn
is giving birth, within a fragile
thin shell, to our death,
and the heedless feet of the summer strangers
trample, stamp surlily upon
our churlish elegy on the parchment of the sand.

Alun Llwyd (translated by Joseph P. Clancy)

The Mesolithic Period

The history of the peninsula begins in the Mesolithic period (c. 10000-4200 BC) and although we have no evidence for human activity earlier than this in the peninsula, there must have been people living here before this time – though they would have been few in number. It should also be pointed out that the peninsula with which we are familiar today, would not have actually formed until around 7000 BC, which unfortunately means that many Mesolithic sites have probably been lost to rising sea levels.

Our evidence for the Mesolithic period in the peninsula consists of scatters of stone tools found at various sites (e.g. Brynrefail farm near Abersoch, St Mary's church, Aberdaron and Ynys Enlli). Such tools would have been used for various tasks such as gathering wild plant foods and butchering and skinning animals. Mention should also be made here of the recent discovery of an important Mesolithic site discovered on Ynys Enlli and a team led by Mark Edmonds has been investigating this further evidence for hunter-gatherers in the peninsula.

Unfortunately, stone tools are often the only evidence we have of Mesolithic people because as hunter-gatherers they would have lived a transitory lifestyle, moving from place to place as they sought out new food sources in the wild. Therefore their settlements were not built with permanence in mind and so, have often been destroyed by later activity.

Julian Heath: Ancient Echoes (2006)

The Oldest Lands of Wales

... to the west of all the hills you will find that Pembrokeshire, Lleyn and Anglesey are singularly of a type: these are the oldest lands of Wales, the ancient ribs and earliest rocks of geologic time, cut only by the little streams which drain these plateaux. These streams have worn steep watercourses down to the creeks of the coast, so that you will find in Pembrokeshire the roads full of sudden descents, the hills turning sharply downward from the plain, sloping to a bridge, and mounting the other side again – a very different kind of thing from the mountain and valley country where the main road winds with the river and the side roads are but precipitous lanes running up amongst the hills.

Over the face of this varied land live the modern generation of the Welshmen of the past. They have learnt a lot from the strange new world, and they have forgotten much that their fathers knew; but they are bred from the same old stock, and no one like a farmer knows how much that counts.

Eiluned and Peter Lewis: The Land of Wales (1937)

Ffynnon Fair

(St Mary's Well)

They did not divine it, but
they bequeathed it to us:
clear water, brackish at times,
complicated by the white frosts
of the sea, but thawing quickly.

Ignoring my image, I peer down
to the quiet roots of it, where
the coins lie, the tarnished offerings

of the people to the pure spirit
that lives there, that has lived there
always, giving itself up
to the thirsty, withholding
itself from the superstition
of others, who ask for more.

R. S. Thomas (1913-2000)

A Round Table

Llŷn is a very extensive hundred, in general flat but interspersed with hills or rocks. The houses of the common people are very mean, made with clay, thatched and destitute of chimneys. Notwithstanding the laudable example of the gentry, the country is in an unimproved state, neglected for the sake of the herring-fishery. The chief produce is oats, barley and black cattle; I was informed that above 3,000 are annually sold out of these parts. Much oats, barley, butter and cheese are exported. The land is excellent for grazing but destitute of trees except about the houses of the gentry.

Descending into an extensive flat, reached Portin-llaen, a fine safe and sandy bay guarded on the west by a narrow headland jutting far into the sea. On part of it are the remains of very strong entrenchments, probably an outpost of the Romans who, as I shall have occasion to mention, had another between this place and Caernarfon.

Separated from this bay by a small headland is that of Nefyn and near to it a small town of the same name, a contributory borough to Caernarfon. This place had been bestowed on Nigel de Lohareyn by the Black Prince, in the 12th year of his principality, and made a free borough. He also gave it a grant of 2 fairs annually and a market on Sunday to which the inhabitants of that part of the Cwmwd Llŷn were obliged to resort.

Here Edward I, in 1284, held his triumph on the conquest of Wales and, perhaps to conciliate the affections of his new subjects, in imitation of our hero Arthur, held a round table and celebrated it with dance and tournament. The concourse was prodigious for not only the chief nobility of England but numbers from foreign parts graced the festival with their presence.

Thomas Pennant (1726-1798): A Tour in Wales

Vortigern's Valley

This was the valley that revealed itself to King Vortigern and his faithful followers. Looking down from the mountains he recognised it as the refuge he had sought over so many weary miles. A king disposessed, he had trekked wounded and dispirited across the land from distant Wessex, what had been his fortunes, had caused the loss of his kingdom and brought him to this inaccessible place? The place that henceforth would bear his name, that of Vortigern's valley and in Welsh Nant Gwrtheyrn.

Vortigern, a Celt, ruled as King of Wessex. His was the first rule to unite the tribes under one leader and as a result he organised the first form of Council in England. The Council was made up of the accepted elders of the various tribes. His aim in uniting the tribes was to discourage persistent attacks by the Picts and the Irish who repeatedly sent out raiding parties to sack and pillage and generally create havoc in the settlements. The scheme proved to be highly successful and was admired by many but it also brought resentment from those who were jealous of his success and popularity.

All went well for him until news reached him of an Irish intent to invade in force. Fearing that he had insufficient forces to quell such an invasion as well as deal with the Picts he decided to seek help from the Jutes, Hengist and Horsa, whom he believed were his friends. In return for their assistance he invited them to settle with their warriors in Thanet. Hardly able to believe their good fortune but delighted, the Jutes readily accepted, seeing it as an ideal opportunity to get a foot-hold in Wessex.

As expected, the Irish attempted to invade but Vortigern's fears and resultant invitation to the Jutes proved unnecessary as he subdued the Irish without their assistance. Regrettably for him that invitation was also to prove to be one of his greatest mistakes and was eventually to cost him his kingdom.

Having settled and gained Vortigern's trust, Hengist, a cunning man, plotted with the Picts to stage an invasion by massing their forces on the border. This accomplished, he hurried with news of the threat to Vortigern, suggesting that a larger force than they could muster would be needed to deal with it and the only remedy would be to bring in more of his men. Vortigern, trusting Hengist implicitly, readily agreed to his suggestion. Hengist, losing no time, immediately brought in a large force of Saxon warriors and kinsmen and also his daughter, Rowena. With this force supporting them the two Jutes had set the stage to gain control and get rid of the King.

Their next move was that of ensuring Vortigern's continued trust and to this end they planned an elaborate banquet in his honour. The banquet took place as arranged and from the Jutes' point of view was a complete success. Wine flowed freely and eventually everyone but themselves became very drunk. At this point Hengist presented his beautiful daughter to the King and he, enchanted by her beauty, fell instantly and deeply in love with her. Without hesitation Vortigern asked Hengist for her hand in marriage adding, 'ask of me what you will and it shall be yours'. Hengist cunningly feigning surprise, replied that he would consider the matter and at once hurried away to consult his advisors. In a short time he returned to inform the King that he would agree to the marriage on condition that he was given the rule of Kent. Vortigern, a man of his word, agreed to the condition without hesitation.

When news of the King's foolhardiness spread throughout the Kingdom those who had resented his skill and courage now jumped at the opportunity to openly criticise him. Hearing of this, the Jutes became confident that the time was ripe to overthrow him. Impatient to achieve his end, Hengist set about picking a fight with the King. He accused him of failing to supply sufficient food and money to support his warriors and threateningly demanded immediate availability of larger supplies. As expected, the King, shocked and distressed and not least by Hengist's manner, denied the accusation. At once Hengist turned nasty and a fight ensued. The fight became a bitter one and continued relentlessly until Vortigern's son Vortimer killed Horsa and as a result Hengist was contained.

Not long afterwards Vortimer died suddenly. By this time the Elders, tired of so much strife and suffering, wanted a lasting peace in the land. Vortigern, too, wanted peace and wanted only to live happily with Rowena whom he had made his wife and with whom he was still deeply in love. Bearing no malice, he readily forgave Hengist his treachery and again offered him his friendship. Hengist eagerly responded, saying that he, too, was weary of conflict and was only too willing to play his part in making every effort to keep the peace.

Agreement seemed finally to have been reached and all was quiet in the kingdom for a time. Regrettably for the King, that peace was to be short lived, for Hengist, treacherous and cunning as ever, had prepared a plan to rid himself of Vortigern once and for all. Calling his men together, he told them of his plan. He explained that he would invite the King and his Elders to a banquet of friendship. At the banquet each Briton was to be seated next to a Saxon and each Saxon was to be armed with a dagger hidden in his shoe. At Hengist's command, they were to rise and slaughter the Elders, but Vortigern, for whom he had other plans, was not to be harmed.

Seeing the invitation as a genuine attempt to further their

friendship, the King happily looked forward to the occasion. The banquet took place and the seating arrangements were accepted with complete trust. Halfway through the feast Hengist signalled to his men and the assault began. Such was the surprise and speed of the attack that the Elders stood no chance of escape and all were slaughtered. Vortigern, helpless and stunned by the carnage, was taken prisoner. Any fears he may have had as to why he alone had been allowed to survive must soon have been confirmed when Hengist played his final card, that of offering Vortigern his freedom in exchange for the rule of Essex and Sussex. The King, horrified by the thought but now a broken man, shamefully agreed.

With nothing left but dishonour and a handful of still loyal subjects, he wandered away, bewildered, into what had become a hostile land, for news of the massacre and his shameful failure had travelled before him. An outcast and hounded by those he had served so well he fled, knowing not where to find refuge. Reaching the Rivals Mountains, he saw beneath him the uninhabited and so peaceful valley and knew that he need travel no more.

How long he survived in the valley is unknown but legend has it that he built a wooden castle on a raised mound above the shore. One night, some years later, a terrible storm broke and a thunderbolt struck the puny castle. The whole structure went up in flames and the deposed King was burned to death.

Whatever the truth of the legend, it is fact that some centuries later a large slab of rough hewn granite was discovered in the valley, inscribed upon it in Celtic form was the name Vortigern. On investigation it was found to be a grave containing the skeleton of a very tall man, which the King was reputed to have been.

The Chronicler Bede wrote a great deal about Vortigern and branded him as a coward. Understandably Bede's opinion was highly prejudiced as Vortigern was not of his faith and had openly rejected his dogma, he preferred a more simple but nonetheless sincere form of belief. Others who wrote at the time and earlier, such as Gildas, respected Vortigern and claimed that he was a well meaning and brave leader.

Eileen M. Webb: This Valley Was Ours (1997)

The Deserted Village

In spite of its history, and in spite of continuing legend, a quarrying community inhabited the place in modern times, and built for themselves stout houses and a school, and a chapel to worship in. But with the coming of the mobile society, it was too isolated, too difficult of access. Their derelict houses, gaping to the sky looked as benighted as any village of the damned. I knew nothing of the story when I found the place that day. It was simply an abandoned city, many of the houses still almost intact in those days, the chapel roofed and windowed, the sheep wandering in and out of doorways. There were unkempt fruit-trees tangled in gardens and there were dark, overhanging rocks above. I wandered about, buried in bracken, ensnared in briars, stared through windows, thunderstruck. What had happened? Why was it an empty world? Where were the ghosts? I didn't dare explore too much, nor stay too long, for I felt that some presence would be sure to come back, to accuse me of trespass, perhaps to trap me there for ever. I turned on my heel, and ran and slithered back down the cliff side to the sea's edge, and never asked anyone about it, never confessed that I'd found it. I dreamt about it though, and treasured it in my secret places, and always meant to return, but never did. It was years later that I first heard anyone else mention the place, and was told its stories. Then it stopped being my place and I wasn't interested in it any longer.

The medieval pilgrims would have moved past Vortigen's bolthole, oblivious to its existence, from

Aelhaearn's church on the far side of Yr Eifl to Beuno's other church at Pistyll on this side. They moved through pestilence and plague, as the saints before them. The powers of darkness, in the shadow of these hills, must have seemed very close. And as they moved on through Llŷn, their path grew narrower. On either side the sea closed in.

R. Gerallt Jones (1934-1999): A Place in the Mind

Nant Gwrtheyrn

Perched on a grassy ledge,
like some rare sea-birds we feel;
learning the language of an endangered species.

And whatever the reasons that brought us,
the sea shelves at the edge
of our thoughts and the mountains
mouse our trivialities. Shaggy, purple head
of the lying yet waiting peninsula.

The wind's descant and harp-curves
of branches, together in penillion.
Candles are toadstools turned into a rage
of horses by Gwydion's flames.
I am dumb: my mind full of knelling
calls of quarrymen, pulled by the waves' ropes.

Wild goats tread the cliff-path
between reality and myth.
Shy and wary behind a twmp:
hear their night-time rock-fall
as they move in to graze
on pastures which pit beyond our step.

I watch the gradual renovation:
my learning tractored across rough ground
and voice beginning to fit the rhythm
of the carpenter as I feel
around and around, the eddying of Yr Iaith.

See, the granite lies in piles of nuggets
where no boat will beach.
High up to the mountain-top
the stone-supports hoist only cloud.
Listen how we talk and how the sea
rolls boulders from its tongue.

Mike Jenkins

The Living Spring

Here, there were pilgrims
born of the waves
kneeling with sunset in their eyes.
Cian, Iestyn, Pedrog and Tudwal
laying down their knotted sticks of hands, they lapped
silence from cold waters.
From a land beyond their vision
where their prayers could reach,
came news which lifted them:
news of a living stream
which flowed without ebbing
and never lost its clarity
however much of washing and drinking.

Gorse-flowers have been extinguished
on the mountainside, Cian
and the stream of Tudwal
has become sluggish with silt,
the rill of Oerddwr

runs dry till moss is white;
orchid and mint are choked
and horsebane strangled by slime.

But listen, Iestyn and Pedrog,
if you eavesdrop you'll discover
that land and water are one.
Creatures of both, the toads,
leap on their web of stones
just as in your time.
Raiding storms from the sea
which besiege the clifflines
did not end with you.

Moses Glyn Jones (translated by Mike Jenkins)

Quarrying for Cymraeg

It seemed like the end of the world,
down the rough track clinging to the cliff-edge,
one skid and we would be hurled
onto the set-out square of the village.
But, she drove down, our faces ghostly-white,
the colour of lovers and legends,
to quarry for the language day and night,
Cymraeg the rock to build roads upon.
We thought we would never return
up that death-lane to another country,
where our lessons might be un-learned
and even granite could snap like a tree.
The stone once shifted upwards on a sled
as words were hoisted into our heads.

Mike Jenkins: Walking on Waste
(Gwasg Carreg Gwalch, 2007)

Sheriffs from Llŷn

In drawing the Caernarvonshire gentry into the public service the Tudors stretched their hand even to distant (but relatively populous) Llŷn. It is a sign of the growing participation of these remoter parts in county affairs that a third of Caernarvonshire's sheriffs during the last twenty years of the century were drawn from Llŷn and Eifionydd, which had supplied not a single one during the first fifty years; and we shall find the same phenomenon in the government of the Church. Some two miles north-west of Pwllheli lay the estate of Bodfel, from which another county family took its name once surnames came into fashion. Until about the middle of the century its record remained undistinguished; then John Wyn ap Hugh took service under the earl of Warwick – soon to achieve notoriety as the duke of Northumberland who virtually ruled England in the later years of Edward VI. He was Warwick's standard bearer when Ket's rebellion was crushed at Mousehold Hill, where, (as Sir John Wyn tells us) 'his hors was slaine under him and himself hurt and yet he upheld the great stander of England'. For this he was richly rewarded with both offices and lands, including some of the former lands of the abbey of Bardsey on the island itself and on the mainland of Caernarvonshire. He was accused of using both office and land to promote piracy, with the island as a depôt for his loot and his public position to shield him from prosecution.

Another son of Llŷn who entered the service of the same earl of Warwick was Griffith ap John of Castellmarch (near Aberdaron) – scion of a very ancient family originating south of the Traeth. His grandfather had been appointed to one of the minor offices in the county hierarchy soon after the Act of Union, and his father became sheriff in 1548. Griffith's service with the earl of Warwick, like John Wyn ap Hugh's, brought with it further advancement: in 1549 he was given the influential post of constable of Conway. All this laid a firm foundation for distinguished and lucrative careers for his sons and grandsons (who took the name of Jones) in the next century. Also near Aberdaron was the fair house of Bodwrda, which gave its name to a family closely akin to the Bodvels. What was the source of the wealth which enabled this ancient but hitherto inconspicuous family to qualify for the office of sheriff in 1584, and some forty years later to rebuild Bodwrda in brick (a rare and long unique building material for so remote a region) is a matter of guesswork; one can only observe that, like their kinsmen of Bodfel, they lived conveniently near the sea! The equally ancient stock of Griffith of Cefnamwlch, some six miles to the north, came into its own in the next century, but it too had supplied a sheriff by 1589. Cefnamwlch lies only a couple of miles from a sequestered shore; a younger son of the house, Captain Hugh Griffith, apprenticed to a London merchant, had for years carried on a profitable privateering business against Spain, and then extended it to less legitimate operations, in which his father participated, as well as his brother-in-law William Jones of Castellmarch, recorder of Beaumaris and a future judge. There were investigations at the court of admiralty, but it does not appear that the dubious gains of the two families were ever disgorged.

A. H. Dodd (1891-1975): A History of Caernarfonshire

Plas yn Rhiw

Plas yn Rhiw, within fairly close proximity to Aberdaron, was for some years the home of the Keating sisters, who restored it and eventually gave it to the National Trust. They were women of passion and vision who played an important role in the communal life of Llŷn.

But the house had an interesting history well before they moved to live there.

Overlooking Ynys Môn, the whole western coast of Wales

and parts of Ireland, it was an ideal spot for Meirion Goch of the royal line of Powys, to settle when he was sent by his grandfather, the king, to watch for marauding Norsemen. It was to him that the Lewis's, the first known owners of the Plas, traced their origins.

Sixteen thirty-four is the earliest date inscribed on the house, and it was probably about this time that the Plas, in its present form, was erected by John Lewis. This would have consisted of the south-western end forming the parlour, the spiral stairs and the western end of the hall on the ground floor, with bedrooms above and a loft for the servants on the top floor. A document copied from the Caernarfonshire Court of Quarter Sessions, is displayed in the house and refers to the son of John Lewis – 'Richard Lewis in Rhiwe' as the owner in 1643.

Nevertheless, the very thick walls of the gable end suggest an earlier building, later incorporated into the Jacobean. Early in the eighteenth century, a *croglofft* cottage was built at right angles to the house, possibly as a dower house. By the nineteenth century, this was used as a bakehouse and laundry. At present it has been restored as a holiday cottage. Later in the eighteenth century, the house itself was extended by the addition of a large kitchen, with a storeroom and another room above. The stairs were moved and a partition erected to give a small parlour as sitting room at the southern end. The removal of the bottom flight of the spiral staircase left an alcove which the Keatings thought at first to be a priest-hole, since Llŷn was one of the last bastions of the Old Religion. There is no evidence for this.

At the beginning of the nineteenth century, the heiress, Jane Ann Lewis, married William Williams. Her daughter, again the heiress, married Captain Lewis Bennet, who soon afterwards set about enlarging the house. The date 1820, together with the initials LMB, was inscribed on a lead weight from one of the sash windows, which the Keatings discovered during their renovations of 1940. About the same time, the roof was raised to provide a second storey attic. The alteration is clearly visible on the outside walls today. A verandah was added to the front of the house; the windows were enlarged and the walls stuccoed to give it the appearance of a Regency manor house.

When Captain Bennet died in 1850, it was his grandson who inherited. He never married and at his death the house passed to his half-brother, thus extinguishing the direct line of succession. Debts accrued, part of the land was sold off and the house itself was sold to a Mr Roberts, whose son let both house and land. One of the tenants of the house was Lady Strickland, who used it for summer holidays. She is credited with planting the box-hedges in the garden, to shelter it from the south-east wind.

The last tenant left in 1922, after which the house and garden fell into disrepair until the Keatings bought them in 1939.

Mary Allen: The Women of Plas yn Rhiw (2005)

Holyhead or Porthdinllaen?

... both Holyhead and Porthdinllaen were candidates for development by Government action as major harbours of refuge as well as packet stations, and the two issues though separate in origin and dealt with by different departments of state, the Admiralty and the Post Office respectively, became confused in the competitive claims of each place, both at the time and in later accounts of the controversy when folklore began to take over.

Porthdinllaen is some fifteen miles to the south west of Caernarfon bar on the north facing coast of the Lleyn peninsula. It is sheltered from the prevailing westerly and south-westerly winds by the peninsula called Trwyn or sometimes Penrhyn Porthdinllaen which projects for about three-quarters of a mile northwards and is in some places less than 200 yards across. Between Trwyn Porthdinllaen and the smaller headland of Penrhyn Nefyn which protects the smaller bay of Porth Nefyn there is a crescent shaped bay, fringed by sand and sheltered by cliffs between 80 and 100 feet high, some one and a quarter miles across and containing about 100 acres of water with an average depth of 30 feet. Within the larger crescent and nestling close under the cliffs is a small cove with a short mole on its northern side. Around the cove are a few cottages, a former inn, White Hall, and a group of houses, the Tŷ Coch Inn and a pier and warehouse, now a private residence. Between the cove and the headland stands the Lifeboat Station which has an honourable record of service since its establishment in 1864.

Stand on the headland on a fine spring or summer evening; behind you on the peninsula are the outlines of an iron age fort, possibly the marine station for the great iron age complex on Tre'r Ceiri on the peak of Yr Eifl (The Rivals) six miles to the east. Behind you again, some four miles to the south stands the peak of the 1200 foot Garn Fadryn which makes a convenient landmark for the approach to Porthdinllaen from seawards. As you walk by the well kept fairways and greens of the golf course which now occupies the peninsula (and one wonders how much the magnificent scenery distracts the players from their serious concern with the game) you will see on the western side the rocky islets, the sharp cliffs and the caves, one of which extends well inland and connects with the surface through what resembles an enormous whale's blow hole. When it is blowing hard you will hear the roar of the sea through it and see the waves throwing cascades of spray high into the air; if you walk to the other side of the peninsula you will see by contrast an almost tranquil sea in the lee of the land. Thomas Rogers, 'Engineer and Light House Builder etc' who was commissioned by W. A. Madocks to report on the suitability of Porthdinllaen as a packet station wrote in a pamphlet published in Dublin in 1807 that in a westerly blow 'the sea is little agitated within the bay or harbour as may be observed by the houses on the shore being built nearly to the high water mark.'

Go back to the headland and watch the sunset; if you are lucky you will see silhouetted against the sun's declining disc the Wicklow Hills. It is tempting to think that our forbears in contemplating the shimmering red-gold path of the sunset on the sea saw in it a symbol of the potential wealth to be gained from capturing the seaway – or should one now say Sealink? – to Ireland.

Stand on Holyhead Mountain, delete from your sight if you can the massive curved breakwater, the ferry terminal and the inner harbour. Look at Salt Island, detach it in your mind's eye from the mainland, and you will see Holyhead Harbour as it was in Lewis Morris' time. Salt Island with its greatest length of some half a mile in a north-south axis provided much the same protection against westerly and south-westerly gales as did Trwyn Porthdinllaen. Instead of the sandy cove there is a muddy tidal creek (now dredged and opened out as the inner harbour). Holyhead Mountain (709 feet) stands out clearly as a mark from seawards; and for good measure Holyhead, too, was recognized by our very early forbears for its natural advantages as a harbour as evidenced by the extensive iron age settlement on Holyhead Mountain and the ancient wall in S. Cybi's churchyard which is reputedly part of a Roman naval station.

The difference between Porthdinllaen and Holyhead lies in the geographical position of each. As the crow flies, or as Rogers put it *in bird line*, Holyhead is 25 miles north of Porthdinllaen and proportionally further from London but the distance of each from Dun Laoghaire (or Kingstown as it was called for the greater part of the period covered by our story) differs by a mere six miles in Holyhead's favour.

It is hardly necessary to labour the point that transport by water is much less energy-consuming than transport over land particularly for bulk cargoes and that is why our oldest ports are situated as far up the estuaries as the ships of the day could navigate; but sea travel is more time-consuming than land travel by a fairly constant factor of three to one, whether one is talking of sailing ships and stage coaches or today's fast ferries and inter-city trains. The ideal packet station, where the speed of the whole journey is the essence, combines the shortest possible sea crossing with the most feasible overland route.

As far as the crossing to Ireland is concerned, 'feasible' is here the operative word; at the beginning of the last century there were formidable barriers still to be surmounted by the transport systems of the day – the uplands and mountains of North Wales. Holyhead could be reached along the traditional conquerors' route from Chester along the narrow coastal plain but at the cost of additional mileage compared with a straight line from London. There were two further hazards on this route, the ferries across the River Conwy and across the Menai Straits. Porthdinllaen was nearer London and only marginally a little further from Kingstown, and thus, *on paper* the stronger contender.

History, however, is not determined by logistics alone, but by their interaction with people and the aspirations and skills available to them, and by events both national and international.

M. Ellis-Williams: Packet to Ireland (1984)

The Pwllheli Union Workhouse

The basic principle of the new Poor Law of 1834 was the gradual abolition of all outdoor relief and the adoption of a rule, like that imposed at Llanbeblig in 1786, that relief should only be given in a properly supervised institution. But in these institutions conditions were to be 'less eligible' than those prevailing in the homes of the lowest grade of independent labourer. This was certainly not the case at Llanbeblig, where the inmates appear from time to time to have been regaled at the ratepayers' expense with meals of pork as well as more commonplace dishes like herrings, 'stirabout' and bread-and-treacle, and to have been warmed with coal fires to the tune of three and a half tons in the year, costing nearly £3; how many Caernarvonshire labourers enjoyed such luxuries? A second principle was the grouping of parishes into Unions; the commissioners had recommended this partly with a view to making possible, by virtue of this wider area, a variety of institutions suited to the needs of different categories of pauper, but this corollary was not embodied in the Act and in fact was very seldom put into effect. Finally, the old Poor Law authorities – the parish vestry, with appeal to the nearest magistrate – were to be replaced by elective Boards of Guardians as the final court of appeal from the overseers throughout the Union; this, it was hoped, would lead to a more uniform and consistent policy and give greater power to those who paid the piper to call the tune . . .

Pwllheli Union was the first to put the Act into full operation – partly, perhaps, because of the high rates with which some of the western parishes were burdened. Its Board of Guardians was elected in 1837 and a workhouse to hold two hundred inmates was built. Ten years later all relief outside the workhouse was stopped. In accordance with the spirit of the Act, conditions were less 'eligible' here than they appear to have been in the old Llanbeblig workhouse. Breakfast and supper consisted in porridge or gruel made of seven ounces per person of oats with buttermilk or water; for dinner, four ounces a head of meat were allowed on Sunday, on other days soup, stew or cheese, with six or seven ounces of bread per head. But the full squalor is revealed only when we learn that no knives or forks were issued until 1900, and then only under pressure from the Local Government Board! The Llanbeblig workhouse had either faded out or did not satisfy the requirements of the Act, but there was naturally opposition to the expense of building a new one, and it needed a judicial order in 1843 to compel the Guardians to act. The new workhouse was at last built in 1846, but it did not have a good name: as late as 1880 it was reported that the bedding remained unchanged for weeks on end, and that the children went about tattered and verminous.

A. H. Dodd (1891-1975): A History of Caernarfonshire

Pen-y-Berth

The British Government had decided to establish a new bombing-school for the Royal Air Force. Several English sites had been considered and spared – Holy Island in Northumberland after a protest in *The Times*, Abbotsbury in Dorset because of its breeding swans – so the Air Ministry decided instead upon Llŷn, a region almost poignantly rich in Welsh memory, entirely Welsh-speaking, proud of the poets, priests, seamen and shipbuilders it had contributed to the history of the nation. The people of Llŷn were horrified, protests poured into London from all parts of Wales, but the Government refused to meet a delegation to discuss the issue, and the Royal Air Force went ahead. The focal point of the range was to be Pen-y-Berth, one of the most storied of the Llŷn homesteads, claiming connections with Owain Glyndŵr himself: by September 1936 this ancient place had been demolished, and the first buildings of the school had been erected.

Just a week after the destruction of Pen-y-Berth three men set fire to the new buildings. They were an unlikely trio of saboteurs. Saunders Lewis we have already met, scholar, poet, playwright, a Catholic convert of passionate views and European loyalties. D. J. Williams was a former miner, a schoolmaster, a writer of short stories, whose round spectacles and Pickwickian eyes made him seem innocence incarnate. And the Revd Lewis Valentine was a Baptist Minister who looked jolly, kind and altogether Christian. Together, at dead of night, these improbable terrorists crept through the perimeter fence of the range, threw petrol over an empty hut, and despite the irritating dampness of D. J.'s matches, set fire to it. It burnt in no time, but hardly had its flames died away than the Revd Mr Valentine, Mr D. J. Williams and Saunders Lewis the playwright were standing before the desk at Pwllheli police station, explaining to a bemused duty officer what they had done (and discussing while they awaited their removal to the cells, so legend says, the sonnets of Robert Williams Parry).

And what they had done was this: they had expressed the Welsh sense of grievance, the old resistance, in a frankly patriotic way – not as an aspect of social reform, but in the older way, for the sake of Wales and Welshness, *er mwyn Cymru*. They were charged in Caernarfon with arson, but the Welsh jury failing to agree, their case was transferred to the Old Bailey in London, where twelve men true, good and English soon saw that they were sentenced to nine months in Wormwood Scrubs. Even Lloyd George was infuriated – 'this is the first Government that has tried Wales at the Old Bailey . . . '

The effect upon young Welshmen was electric – 'it is difficult now,' wrote the critic R. M. Jones thirty years later, 'to imagine what a thrilling impact this happening had' – and since the Second World War the endemic and almost organic sense of Welsh protest has coalesced above all around the nationalist idea.'

Jan Morris: Wales: Epic Views of a Small Country (1984)

A Matter of Life and Death

Speaking in defence of the charges brought against both himself and his two fellow patriots at Caernarfon Crown Court in October 1936 Saunders Lewis was passionate in his arguments.

. . . if you examine our record, you will find that our works, our programme, our propaganda have been entirely constructive and peaceful. There has never been any appeal to mob instincts. In fact, our leadership has been accused of being too highbrow and academic. I have repeatedly and publicly declared that the Welsh nation must gain its political freedom without resort to violence or to physical force. It is a point I wish to re-affirm today. And I submit to you that our action in burning the Penrhos aerodrome proves the sincerity of this affirmation. Had we wished to follow the methods of violence with which national minority movements are sometimes taunted, and into which they are often driven, nothing could have been easier than for us to ask some of the generous and spirited young men of the Welsh Nationalist Party to set fire to the aerodrome and get away undiscovered. It would be the beginning of methods of sabotage and guerilla turmoil. Mr Valentine, Mr D. J. Williams and I determined to prevent any such development. When all democratic and peaceful methods of persuasion had failed to obtain even a hearing for our case against the bombing range, and when we saw clearly the whole future of Welsh tradition threatened as never before in history, we determined that even then we would invoke only the process of law, and that a jury from the Welsh people should pronounce on the right and wrong of our behaviour.

The Judge interrupted: 'You are telling the jury – and I say this in your own interests – the reasons why you took the steps you did and burnt down the aerodrome; and I tell you that that is no excuse in law, and that the more you persist in telling the jury your ideas about Welsh nationalism and Welsh culture, the less excuse there is for having committed this act. So far your argument has been totally irrelevant to the charge.'

Mr Lewis answered: I thought I was speaking on it the whole time. I am sorry. *And he continued with his address:* We ourselves, public men in Wales and leaders of the Welsh Nationalist Party, fired these buildings and timbers. We ourselves reported the fire to the police. We have given the police all the help we could to prepare the case against us. Is that the conduct of men acting 'feloniously and maliciously'? I submit that we are in this dock of our own will, not only for the sake of Wales, but also for the sake of peace and unviolent, charitable relations now and in the future between Wales and England.

It is charged against us that our action was 'unlawful'. I propose to meet that charge by developing an argument in four stages. First, I shall show with what horror the building of a bombing range was regarded by us and by a great number of Welsh people in every part of Wales. Secondly, how patiently and with what labour and at what sacrifice we tried and exhausted every possible way of legitimate persuasion to prevent the building of the bombing range. Thirdly, how differently the protests and remonstrances of Wales and Welsh public men were treated by the English Government, compared with similar protests, though less seriously grounded protests, made in England in the same period. Fourthly, I shall try to put before you the dilemma and the conflict of obedience in which the Government's cruelty placed the leaders of the crusade against the bombing range, and the limits to the rights of the English State when it transgresses the moral law and acts in violation of the rights of the Welsh nation.

In an English pamphlet stating the case against the bombing school in Lleyn, Professor Daniel has expressed with pregnant brevity the heart-felt fear of all thoughtful Welshmen.

The Judge again interrupted: 'What Professor Daniel said has no bearing on the case. I only say this in your own interest, that if you go on addressing the jury as you have done, you are – so far from putting up any defence – making the case against you worse.'

Mr Lewis continued: It is the plain historical fact that, from the fifth century on, Lleyn has been Welsh of the Welsh, and that so long as Lleyn remained unanglicized, Welsh life and culture were secure. If once the forces of anglicization are securely established behind as well as in front of the mountains of Snowdonia, the day when Welsh language and culture will be crushed between the iron jaws of these pincers cannot be long delayed. For Wales, the preservation of the Lleyn Peninsula from this anglicization is a matter of life and death.

That, we are convinced, is the simple truth. So that the preservation of the harmonious continuity of the rural Welsh tradition of Lleyn, unbroken for fourteen hundred years, is for us 'a matter of life and death'. I have said that my professional duty is the teaching of Welsh literature. My maternal grandfather was a minister of religion and a Welsh scholar and man of letters. He began his ministerial career in Pwllheli. He wrote the greatest Welsh prose work of the nineteenth century, *Cofiant John Jones Talsarn* (*The Biography of John Jones of Talsarn*). One of the most brilliant chapters in that book is the seventh chapter, which is a description of the religious leaders of Lleyn and Eifionydd in the middle of the nineteenth century. It is impossible for one who had blood in his veins not to care passionately when he sees this terrible vandal bombing range in this very home of Welsh culture. On the desk before me is an anthology of the works of the Welsh poets of Lleyn, *Cynfeirdd Lleyn, 1500-1800* (*Early Poets of Lleyn, 1500-1800*), by Myrddin Fardd. On page 176 of this book there is a poem, a *cywydd*, written in Penyberth farmhouse in the middle of the sixteenth century. That house was one of the most historic in Lleyn. It was a resting-place for the Welsh pilgrims to the Isle of Saints, Ynys Enlli, in the Middle Ages. It had associations with Owen Glyn Dŵr. It belonged to the story of Welsh literature. It was a thing of hallowed and secular majesty. It was taken down and utterly destroyed a week before we burnt on its fields the timbers of the vandals who destroyed. And I claim that, if the moral law counts for anything, the people who ought to be in this dock are the people responsible for the destruction of Penyberth farmhouse.

Ed. Alun R. Jones and Gwyn Thomas:
Presenting Saunders Lewis (1983)

'The Great Mysteries of Life'

In his autobiographical book, My Brother and I, *William George, brother to Lloyd George, recalls their formative years in the Llanystumdwy area.*

The creed of the church of which my sister, my brother and myself successively became members, was both simple and comprehensive in character. Each applicant for membership of the church confessed his or her belief in God, Father, Son and Holy Ghost, and his or her determination to follow Jesus Christ through life. On the strength of this confession the candidate was baptized by immersion 'in the presence of many witnesses', and was afterwards accepted into membership of the church. The only ritual indulged in was the Communion Service or 'the breaking of bread' every Lord's Day, in remembrance of Him. A ritual of such extreme austerity and simplicity as this could not be sustained as a perennial and permanent influence in life unless in the first instance it was based on an intense conviction of its rightness, and unless also that conviction stood the test of experience in the long-drawn-out battle of life.

My brother was baptized in a little brook running in front of the Penymaes Chapel which was converted into a baptistry on this and similar occasions. The important event took place on the 7th February, 1875, Uncle Lloyd being, as usual, the officiating minister. Dafydd was then in the thirteenth year of his life. He remained a very active member of the church whilst we lived at Llanystumdwy and later on during the Criccieth period. In after life politics became a full-time job for him and London had to become his headquarters, nevertheless, he never lost complete touch with the church at Criccieth, of which he was a full member to the very end.

A question which might very fairly be asked at this stage is this: Is there any evidence to show that Lloyd George's acceptance of the simple creed of the Church of Christ was anything more than formal; something he did without much thought under the influence of the dominating personality of his revered uncle? I think there is ample evidence from contemporary documents in his own handwriting, as well as from his actions in early manhood, to prove that his professions of faith were sincere and deep-seated. And I will quote chapter and verse from his diaries and original writings in support of the conviction to which I have just given expression.

Among the numerous meditations which my brother reduced to writing in his early days is a substantial essay on 'Life'. This is marked as having been written by him in the year 1883, when he was twenty years old. This essay, coupled with a large number of notes written by him about the same time demonstrate very clearly that during this period he was taking religious belief, in all its aspects, very seriously, and was deliberately putting on record the conclusions at which he had then arrived regarding the great mysteries of life, here and hereafter.

William George: My Brother and I (1982)

Us Against Them

. . . in 1890 David Lloyd George, standing as a radical Liberal for the Caernarfon Boroughs in his first parliamentary election, found himself opposing Hugh Ellis-Nanney, who was not only the squire of Lloyd George's own village, Llanystumdwy, but had also been Agent to Lord Penrhyn of Penrhyn Castle and the Bethesda quarries.

It was like a Morality. Ellis-Nanney lived in Plas Gwynfryn, a huge mock-Gothic mansion which he had recently built on a hill above the village, surrounded by a glorious park: Lloyd George had grown up in a small terrace house in the village street, almost opposite the Feathers Inn. It was street against park, Welsh-speaking Baptist cobbler's ward against English-speaking Anglican agent of Mammon – Us Against Them with a vengeance. Lloyd George himself embellished the images in a famous speech. 'I see that one qualification Mr Nanney possesses,' he cried, 'is that he is a man of wealth, and that the grand disqualification in my case is that I am possessed of none . . . the Tories have not yet realized that the day of the cottage-bred man has at last dawned!'

He was right. Not only did the cottage-bred man win that particular contest, but all over Wales the people succeeded to political power. The squirearchy was swept from its seats of authority, and the county councils were dominated by men of the middle classes, farmers, doctors, shopkeepers, ministers, small businessmen. First as a stronghold of Liberalism, then of Labour, the country has been left of centre ever since, and since Lloyd George's day all its authentic heroes, every one, have been bold and often militant radicals – if not cottage men exactly, certainly not men of the Plas. It is apt that Ellis-Nanney's great house of Gwynfryn, having been in its time a nunnery, an old people's home and un unsuccessful hotel, is now only a burnt-out ruin on its commanding hilltop site: while the cobbler's cottage in the village below has a commemorative slab upon it, and is portrayed on picture postcards.

Jan Morris: Wales: Epic Views of a Small Country (1984)

Welsh Incident

*(In the early hours of September 3rd, 1997,
a giant turtle was found dead, on the
shoreline at Cricieth)*

The Cambrian News reporter's car
blocks the lane down to the shore.

Someone plays the bagpipes
where the last field meets the sea.

But for the randomness of the tide
she'd still be gracing the waters
of a century as it drowned.

Armour-plated, run aground,
a creaturely grief mourns her end.

Two elderly, village paparazzi
circle the wreckage, take snaps
before the oceanographers descend.

Paul Henry

At Tre'r Ceiri

There were giants in Llŷn in those days, and they lived on
                                                this mountain
Behind these drystone walls piled high to keep secrets and
                                                hutch holy
Things from the god-searching singing wind off the sea
                                                twelve fields below.

The peak of Yr Eifl towered over them, more psalmist than
                                                guardian,
For it lifted their eyes to the fierce sun drowning beyond
                                                Ireland
And gave them scale, while the rubble trickling slowly down
                                                the scree slopes

Taught them comparative weight and the fragility of all
                                                flesh.
They were invincible in all other respects. So they stood gods

Among men, gods of power and hate, gods who looked
                                    down on their people

In purest contempt for that they were weak and small and
                                                subservient,
And for that they worshipped, and lifted up their mute eyes
                                            in their turn,
And for that they drew their water from deep in St
                                    Aelhaearn's well.

Up on Tre'r Ceiri water came from a spring which sang
                                        below ground
And emerged blinking. They never enclosed it, or put stones
                                            round it,
Or (*O fons Bandusiae*) cut any kid's throat on an altar.

There was no need, the stones were sufficient protection.
                                            The walls now
Are ruinously splayed, but the stream still flows, and the
                                            well is full.

And at the mountain's foot still swings the eternal eroding
                                                sea.

                                        Brian Morris

93

Penyberth

'Beauty,' whispered the leaves to the night,
and the night to the moon, and the moon to the wind.
'Beauty,' cried the wind across the moor,
'There's a fire in Llŷn.'

'Justice,' was the moor's verdict to the rock,
and the rock's to the rain, and the rain's to the sea.
'Justice,' moaned the sea to the strand,
'There's a fire in Llŷn.'

'That's a crime,' said England to the jurors,
and the jurors to the judge.
'That's a crime,' said the judge, 'and the punishment's harsh
for a fire in Llŷn.'

'Not guilty,' murmured the sun to the dale,
and the dale to the stream and the stream to the glen.
'Not guilty,' wept the glen to the dew,
'of a fire in Llŷn.'

'A vineyard was placed in my care,' he said,
'I myself must tend it,
and a generation will rise like a phoenix from the ashes
of the fire in Llŷn.'

Gwynn ap Gwilym (translated by Joseph P. Clancey)

Ynys Enlli

Island of the Blest

Peninsulas are like mountains: they lead you on. Once half-way you must get out to the end. And that is what you feel when you are as far down the Llŷn Peninsula as Pwllheli, in that wrist of lowland that cuts through the mountains to the north coast at Nefyn. There you begin to sense the strong shape of this muscular forearm that jabs south-west into the Atlantic. Now it is but a dozen miles to the end. With every mile the land gets barer, trees and hedges diminishing all the way west into the windswept half-clenched fist whose thumb thrusts south beyond Abersoch to hook round the bay called Porth Neigwl (Hell's Mouth). West of Porth Neigwl truncated fingers push bluntly into the waves: and that is almost the end of Llŷn and the last of north Wales, but not quite. For beyond the fist, beyond two miles of water, a Precambrian finger-tip lies parted from the rest, a five-hundred-foot high rock heaving itself out of the sea as smooth as a rolling dolphin. This is Ynys Enlli which the Vikings named Bardsey.

Seen from the end of the peninsula it might be a desert island, for the brackeny, mountainous back it turns upon the world conceals all sign of habitation. All the same, if you go there do not fancy yourself as a pioneering island-explorer. For whether you are saint or sinner, the number of your kind to have crossed that way before you is certainly legion.

You cannot just skim over to Bardsey in a granite trough or on a green sod as the saints of old used to cruise around on their pious occasions. Mortals of less than saintly stature have always had to find a boat at Aberdaron, and still do. For the pilgrims and holy men of centuries there have been those final exhilarating miles of narrowing roads and widening skies as the last windy headlands, changing with every bend and rise of the way, have taken their final shape. Wherever

95

they came from – and many a local fragment of Ancient Trackway or Pilgrims' Way lettered archaically on the map of Wales seems to point Bardseywards – all their paths converged here at Aberdaron. All descended the last hill to this last village, which until the motoring age remained an almost unknown huddle of fishermen's cottages round an ancient sea-edge church.

The holiday-makers have Aberdaron now, but you have only to turn from the two or three hotels and tea-shops to the changeless curve of the shore, the surviving old low cottages and the salt-sprayed gravestones, to get a strong sense of the past, of the near-tragic life of fisherfolk struggling against poverty and the sea. A century ago a traveller described Aberdaron as 'a miserably poor village'. Today it looks prosperous, but it is still clustered small enough in its little valley along the Daron not to have lost the village charm. They have not yet modernised the humpy bridge or tidied up the alexanders that adorn odd corners in May with their yellow umbels. Let us pray that enough saintly magic still holds in these fingers of Celtic land to forbid the road-straighteners and verge-sprayers for generations yet.

Though you are going to the island in a motorboat you have to respect the six-knot tides of Bardsey Sound. Tides do not change and the waves that try to claw out the dead through Aberdaron's churchyard walls are the same as those that have given pause to Bardsey pilgrims all through time. There is still scrambling into an open boat and poling through the breakers to calmer water before setting of sail or starting of engine. Then away to the open sea and an empty horizon; for not until you clear the bay and begin to feel the Atlantic under you do you see Bardsey quickly race into view round the point. Soon you are across and Bardsey's razorbills and guillemots are whirring down at you from the cliffs and skimming just past the boat, and kittiwakes are showering daintily off their ledges and clangouring round you with voices surprisingly deep for small gulls. Then you are gliding between narrow rocks into the only landing cove, leaping ashore in the ancient way and gathering your possessions on to the beach before you follow the road, the only road, the pilgrims' road.

William Condry (1918-1998): Welsh Country Essays

Thick With Bones

In the late evening, as we sat on the grassy parapet that runs along the northern coast; among flowers, sea-pinks and vernal squills, we saw the young man we had watched earlier in the day near the monastery, disappearing round the mountain with a bucket for gulls' eggs.

At this northern end are black sea caverns. Above the caves the rock is white and worked over in raised veins, polished and fine as ivory. Some of these rock-veins were thin as spider web, others were thick as human arteries. The stone would seem to be composed of petrified tissues, skin, muscle, delicate bones. We ran our fingers over the filigree patterns. Falling to our knees, we touched the remains of our ancestors. Or their sculptured memorials in stone; their ivory-bright bird-bone perfection, the metamorphosed flesh. A valley of sun-whitened skeletons seen through a reducing mirror.

Why this preoccupation with stone, the framework of the earth? While turning over the soil here, a man might philosophise like the gravediggers in Hamlet. The second clown asks a riddle: 'Who builds stronger than a mason, a shipwright or a carpenter?'

And the first clown answers: 'A grave-maker; the houses that he makes last till doomsday.'

In every part of the island which is free of stone, the spade strikes against human thigh and breast-bone. In an island of only four hundred and forty-four acres, with half of that mountain and with reputedly twenty thousand saints buried there, it is understandable that certain areas of the earth should be thick with bones.

Under the eastern height men turn the remains of their ancestors when they dig; forking them over happily under the wide sky-benediction; for these are the bones of men who fulfilled themselves, who found realisation of visions in a fragment of land left miraculously to the air when other portions of this mountain range were submerged in the Pleistocene Age.

We turned southwards, walking to Ogof Lladron, where in a cirque of rock that on one side rises to a saddle, on the other to overhanging cliff, lies a snug and secret anchorage. I could imagine the French smugglers putting in here, swart men in stocking-caps and ear-rings, carrying their cargo of liquor up the precipice. Delightedly, the welcoming islanders used to guide them up to their farms, with talk of roast goose and duck; their eyes on the wine flagons.

A rough grassy track runs the whole way along the west side. While we walked there I mused over the lonely man we had left behind us in the house. He was like someone uprooted too violently, a man out of his place; highly strung and too unstable for this mode of life.

Friedrich began to tell me of his own loneliness, partly from over-burdened emotions, partly because for a few days he was to be out of the world, simplicity and peace loosening his tongue.

In the south, on the black rock of Pen Dinmor, Arthur of the Round Table is said to have been shipwrecked. The boat was lost but the king was saved. The legend has it that the king with torn breast, his royal garments salt-caked and stained, was dragged from the hungry sea by unknown hands and carried inland to the holy fathers, who tended his ragged wounds.

We caught sight for a moment of a tawny cat, one of those domestic animals left behind by families that had moved out. At this time, many homeless cats lived in the gullies of the south end. Island cats quickly revert to the wild, with many rabbits and birds for the hunting, and with much space in which to move freely, except for the danger of gins and snares.

This is a land that hoards its past and merges all of time in the present. The cargo boat that was salvaged last year off Maen Bugail, whose coal cargo will keep the island in fuel for the next twenty years; the illicit sweet wine of France; the shipwreck of Arthur; are of equal importance and freshness. It might be said that what happened here yesterday has taken on the colour of a long-past event, so timeless do happenings appear to be; as if the drama had been written long ago, and we who come by chance to the island play our parts that were designed for us, walking on to the stage at the twitch of a string held in the firm hand of the master.

Puppet strings took me by the hair-roots, drawing me back to the house in the quiet dusk; I had a sense of being forcibly drawn into the life of this elusive world.

It was almost dark by this time. A man in a peaked cap was sitting behind the door, his chair drawn back against the wall. The man had pale ginger hair and a white exhausted face.

'This is Merfyn, one of the lighthouse keepers,' said our host.

An hysterical, high-pitched laugh came from the mask behind the door. It was just possible to see his hands falling limply between his knees, from which hung a cloth bag holding full milk bottles.

After supper, when the two of us were alone, Hopkinson told me something of himself.

'I was brought up by foster-parents. Then I studied the law; while preparing for my examinations, I began to drink a lot of whisky and absinthe. I married Alice, and persuaded her to come here, overlooking that she has an Irish temper, and that she needs to go to a palais de dance every Saturday night. How she hates the sea! But real blind hatred. Now, she's gone off to the mainland to stay with her mother. I'm riding her on a loose rein in the hope that some day she will become resigned to this place.'

He paused to brood, with hunched shoulders.

'Last year, I threw up my law studies, and took this farm

with the Levens's. We arrived in December, after a terrible crossing in which Alice lay flat on her back in the bottom of the boat. The house was no comfort; the bedrooms and living-room walls were running with moisture. The sheets and blankets felt like snails' beds. We were cut off from the mainland for four weeks after the day we arrived, and had to live on corned beef and potatoes. By the end of that time, Alice would not eat any more tinned meat. The islanders were not particularly friendly, either.'

Brenda Chamberlain (1912-1971): Tide Race

No Reptiles

No reptile is ever seen in this island, except the common water lizard. None of the inhabitants ever saw in it a frog, toad, or snake of any kind. – Till about fourteen years ago, no sparrows had been known to breed here: three nests were, however, built during the same spring, and the produce have since completely colonized the place.

There are here but eight houses, although the number of inhabitants is upwards of seventy. Two or three of the principal of these rent the island of lord Newborough. They pay for it a hundred guineas a year, and have their land tythe free, and are also freed from taxes and rates of every description. They keep about twenty horses, and near thirty cows. All the former, though greatly overstocking so small a place, are absolutely necessary, on account of the great labour required in carrying up the seaweeds from the coast for manure.

The sheep are small, and, on the approach of a stranger, as Mr Jones informs me, they squall not much unlike hares. Their activity is very remarkable. In the year 1801, Mr Jones had one of them on his farm at Aberdaron, that had twice ventured through the sea, though the channel is three miles across, and regained the island. The inhabitants train their dogs to catch them, but if the sheep once gain the rocks, they bid defiance to every attempt for the time, as, rather than suffer themselves to be seized, they will plunge from thence into the sea. At the time of the year when the females usually drop their offspring, the inhabitants watch them every day, and before these are able to follow their dams, they mark them in the ears: they then suffer them to range at liberty. Without this attention, from the extreme wildness of the animals, the owners would never be able to distinguish their respective property. Some few of the sheep of the island, from having been rendered tame when young, are more easily managed. These alone submit to be folded in the evenings.

William Bingley (1774-1823): North Wales,
delineated from two excursions

'The Money Bogey'

When the *Beacon* left the Skerries she steered south past the Stack Rocks where the Trinity House flag was hoisted up in our honour and then stood away across Carnarvon Bay for Bardsey Island. Here was another Mecca towards which I had long been fain to make a pilgrimage.

Bardsey is an island separated from the land by a tide-rip even more terrible than than of the Skerries. It was the last stronghold of Christianity in the form introduced into Britain under Roman rule (as opposed to that brought in later by Augustine). The ruin on the island is that of the Benedictine convent which supplanted the Celtic settlement. Since the religious *débâcle* of the sixteenth century, a farming community had collected round the empty monastery, ruled by the headman appointed by the lay impropriator and styled King, this being a shred of the authority properly belonging to the Abbot of Bardsey.

And now, after so many years of longing, I was set comfortably ashore by the ship's gig. But, no sooner did I put foot on land than insight became opaque once more and the money bogey obsessed me. I wandered about among the fields and grassy mounds of that famous islet where, they say, no rabbit can excavate without disturbing the bones of the saints. I wandered past the grey ruins of the old Benedictine abbey thinking not of saints in the past but ways and means in the future.

Edmund Vale (1889-1969): Straw Into Gold

Vespers

The pulse of this place: weather, wings
the stumbling, persistent hum
of bees in late-flowering heather
and plainsong, pacing footsteps;
it is the swish, the shiver and fall
of the swathe to the scythe,
the dry stutter of tractors
and the white mare's hourlong tramp
round the *dyrnwr*, the thwock and splash
of butter coming; chapel bell
and foghorn
and the shipping forecast
three times a day; diesel-throb that turns
the light held level in its bath of mercury;
the swing of waves and the surge and tick
of young in the womb,
the push of men and the trudge of women
carrying milk, carrying water, carrying wood and children
born and unborn.

Nellie gathering her washing from the gorse
behind the school hoods a hand over her eyes
to scan the south-west
or choughs that preach the free church of the air.

She is missing her daughters and fretting for
the album in a ransacked flat in Kuwait City –
pictures of the girls as babies, picnics
above the tree line in the Himalaya, faces of friends
forever now a world away. And wondering
how she will pick up the reins, where to point
the plot of her life.

This wide horizon constantly reminds us
we are all at sea, withdrawn;
larvae of ourselves suspended
ghosts of our own futures
that move towards us like drifting clouds
filling the mind with mist or startling
with sudden sculptured decision.
Some of us perhaps were refugees
or waiting to float free
but we all go back, remembering
this place and time, our bonded fellow travellers
as background, or a break, or a wise dream;
gathering images to pile up round us
as if they'd work like walls in winter.

In the hayloft he has made a bower
of exotic junk (seal's teeth strung
as necklaces, bright stones and bones and shells)
Prof hunches over latest statistics
for pitfall and sweep-net catches. *I have*
he writes, *an inordinate fondness*
for beetles. They comprise thirty percent
of all known species. He reaches for the glass
(vermouth's all gone) and, sliding down
seas of his mind's making, replays
surfing the Sound on a single wave
in a boat moonlit to a chariot of silver . . .

A raven croaks and rises from the crag
where the women used to watch
the island boat, their menfolk going and returning.
Fulmars surf the air, stiff-winged.
While we sit here, the world can change.
The raven sneers and chuckles, and wheeling high
towards mainland fields, choughs scream:
we must not let these clarities
crystalise into the one place
rooted at the centre of the world
lest we make exiles of our mainland selves,
turn dry husks spinning in the web
nostalgia weaves and uses
to suck us into blurring.

Scoop-shapes in the mountain slope
show the scrape of the wind's fingernails.
Round the back, the three paths narrow;
waves wink and beckon: each deck
of this tilting ship has its own catwalk,
its companionway above the water.

Henllwyn: old grove, copse drowned perhaps
in the melting of the glacier that pushed
together this muddle of rock we call Enlli,
this single coherent spot
in the slow crawl of mountains
where we seem not so much to live as to be
lived in, moved by wind and sea and moving clouds
all the bright enigmas of our world.

King's men swing ashore with oaths and axes.
The brothers who have stayed to witness
watch calmly. The last of the gold
the silver pyx and reliquary
are safe in the earth by the spring
in the rock near the Abbot's House.

They have rehearsed the rote of older raids
and returns, and vowed no flinching
when the smashing starts.

Moorhen run between the brandished blades
of iris as the peregrine moth-flutters by.
Seals grunt and mutter and exult, a congregation
getting the *hwyl*, with the cries
of gulls and lambs and Christian children
playing in the hour before they sleep.

It holds the sea in the crook of its arm
this island, blending and letting
difference shine: the gaudy barber's pole
of the lighthouse, the Sea-Truck's bird-yellow
beckoning the eye to the *Storws* roof
lichened like an old tree-trunk.
For generations, its door has been shut
when all the boats are safely home.
Inside, old rope hibernates in lazy coils.
By the limekiln, you might overhear
the drifting ghost of a tin whistle tune.

A single heron hunches stealthily
where water, mirror-calm, throws back
a band of lighthouse red across the bay.

Christine Evans

In Bardsey Sound

(Hilaire Belloc's The Cruise of the Nona *describes a journey by sea around part of the British coastline)*

I looked at the Carnarvonshire coast there close at hand, the sinking lines of the mountains as they fell into the sea, and I discovered myself to be for the first time in my life entirely indifferent to my fate . . .

Anyhow, here I was in Bardsey Sound, with many deaths moving over the howling fury of the sea, and not one of them affecting me so much as a shadow passing over a field.

The end of that adventure was odd and unreasonable – as things will be at sea. It was perhaps because we had been buffeted and pushed into some edge of the conflict between wind and water where the tide runs slacker; or it was perhaps because the wind had risen still higher. But, at any rate, after three separate raids forward (in the second of which we were very nearly out of our peril and into smooth water), and as many set-backs (one of which got us into the worst violence we had yet suffered) the *Nona*, in a fourth attempt (it was her own, not ours – we could do nothing but keep her, as best we might, to her course), slipped out and reached an eddy beyond the tide. For a moment it was very difficult to keep her to it, she slewed round; but then again she got her head southerly, and we found ourselves running past the great Black Rock which stands there – the Carrig Dhu – and marks the smooth water beyond the edge of the tide.

We breathed again; and as I took her on through an easy sea, close under the land with not too much strain upon the helm (for the high shore now broke the gale), I was free to look over my right shoulder and watch, passing away behind us, further and further, the hell of white water and noise, through which we had barely come to safety.

Danger keeps men awake and makes ·them forget necessity, but with this relief, our fatigue came upon us. My friend and I had now been awake for some twenty-five or twenty-six hours, and it was time for sleep.

We got the poor *Nona* which had behaved so well, up into a lonely little bay where was an old abandoned mine working, but no other sign of man. The Welshman with us told it was good holding ground; we let go the anchor and stowed sail. I remember how I fell half asleep as I stretched the cover over the mainsail boom and yard and tied it down at the after end. The gale still blew, yet, as it seemed, more steadily and less fiercely. There was no danger of dragging. We were well under the lee of the land. I gave one look, under the violent but clear morning sky, to seaward before I went below; and there I saw how, at a certain distance from the land, in a long line, the white water began. It was like being in a lagoon, like being protected by a bank from the sea outside; but really it was only the effect of the lee of the land making a belt of smooth water along shore. Then we all lay down to sleep and slept till evening.

Hilaire Belloc (1870-1953): The Cruise of the Nona

Dying By Succession

During the violent struggles between the Welsh and English, it was styled by the poets the Sanctuary, or Asylum of the Saints, and it was sometimes denominated the Isle of Refuge. Some of these poets assert that it was the cemetery of *twenty thousand saints*! The reputed sanctity of this island induced the religious to resort to it from many very distant parts of the country.

It has been asserted by several writers that Roderic Moelwynog, prince of North Wales, first founded here a monastery some time in the eighth century. He might perhaps rebuild or enlarge it, but there are good grounds, from Welsh manuscripts, for supposing that there was a religious house in this island of a much more early date.

There is an old legend yet extant, written in Monkish Latin, which assures us that the Almighty had entered into a particular covenant with Laudatus, the first abbot of Bardsey, in return for the piety of his monks. This granted to all the religious of the monastery of Bardsey, the peculiar privilege of dying according to seniority, the oldest always going off first. By this privilege it is stated, that every one knew very nearly the time of his own departure. The following is a translation of it;– 'At the original foundation of the monastery of this island, the Lord God, who attendeth to the petitions of the just, at the earnest request of holy Laudatus, the first abbot, entered into a covenant with that holy man, and miraculously confirmed his promise, unto him and his successors, the abbots and monks, for ever, while they should continue to lead holy and religious lives, that they should die by succession, that is, that the oldest should go first, like a shock of corn ripe for the sickle. Being thus warned of the approach of death, each of them, therefore, should watch, as not knowing at what exact hour the thief might come; and, being thus always prepared, each of them by turns should lay aside his earthly form. God, who is ever faithful, kept this covenant, as he formerly did with the Israelites, inviolable, until the monks no longer led a religious life, but began to profane and defile God's sanctuary by their fornications and abominable crimes. Wherefore, after this, they were permitted to die like other men, sometimes the older, sometimes the younger, and sometimes the middle-aged first: and being thus uncertain of the approach of death, they were compelled to submit to the general laws of mortality.

Thomas Pennant (1726-1798): A Tour in Wales

The Strongest Man

Tomos Jones spent sixty years of his life on Ynys Enlli, having been born at the end of the nineteenth century. During frequent conversations with him in old age Jennie Jones transcribed some of his memories. These appeared in book form in 1964 in a translation by Gwen Robson.

One of the strongest men on the island was William Huws. Wil Huws he was called. *Duwc annwyl*! there was a giant of a man for you. All the Enlli men were strong at that time, but Wil Huws was the strongest. One of his hands was as big as two ordinary hands. No one dared to cross him because no one could stand up to him. He was a cousin of my father's. He has been buried since many years in 'Mynwent y Seintiau' (the Graveyard of the Saints).

Are there any saints buried there, I can hear you asking. Yes, indeed. The island is called 'Ynys y Seintiau' (Island of the Saints). There are twenty thousand buried there, all over the island and their bones in every corner of it. When ploughing the fields, many skulls and bones come to light – brought up by the ploughshare.

Wil Huws was a farmer and a fisherman, the same as every other man there. The Enlli men had big strong boats that were able to withstand any storm. At the time of catching herring, the men used to be away for days. They had a loft above some stable in Porthdinllaen where they used to clean and salt the herring. After a good catch of herring they used to bring them to the loft, and after cleaning and salting, like I said, would pack them tightly in wooden casks, then send them to various markets. They would send them to Anglesey, Chester, Liverpool and many other places.

One man would usually go with them, and bring the money back to be divided amongst all the fishermen.

* * *

One day he was ploughing in a field above the sea. On the rocks below he saw a big white sack full of something. He left the horses in the field and went down to the rocks. He had clogs on his feet. When he got to the sack, he saw that it was a sack of wheat flour. He lifted it and threw it over his shoulder, and carried it up the rocks safely. How much, would you guess, was the weight of that sack of wheat flour? Two hundred and eighty two pounds. There's a feat for any man.

Jennie Jones: Tomos the Islandman (1964)

'A Convenient Place for Pirates'

In the Calendar of Wynn Papers, Bardsey is described as 'a very convenient place for pirates'. During the 16th century, pirates George Morgan and Nicholas Hookes, and local landowners used the islands of Bardsey and Tudwal as their headquarters. One of these landowners was John Wyn ap Huw, of Bodfel, near Pwllheli (d.1576), who was described as 'chief captain of the pirates of Ynys Enlli [Bardsey]', in a complaint made to the Star Chamber in 1569. He had fought with the Duke of Northumberland's forces in 1549, and had received Bardsey as a reward for his efforts. The island became a centre for pirates to relax after weeks at sea, and a place where they could buy food and drink and ship's supplies such as ropes, ready for their next raids. It was also used to store their stolen goods. John Bodfel and his network would sell these goods in markets and fairs in places as far away as Chester, and because of his good connections with those in authority, he could ensure that the pirates would not be apprehended. But pirates were not always successful in hanging onto their booty.

When Captain Thomas Wolfall brought a shipload of grain, which he had seized in the English Channel, to Llŷn in 1563, John Bodfel boarded her and helped the captain to sell the cargo, as he could not speak Welsh. And when searchers came on board, to try to seize the grain, John Bodfel and another landowner, William Glynne, sent them away, saying that they had more authority than the searchers. One of the Griffiths of Cefnamwlch also went on board to try to claim the grain, but Wolfall said that he had a letter from the Earl of Warwick, giving him permission to attack foreign ships. When John Griffiths asked to see the letter, Wolfall told him that there was no point as the letter was in French. Griffiths then said he would take it a local squire, who could read that language, but, somehow, Wolfall could not find the letter.

John Griffiths appealed to the authorities for permission to seize the grain, but he was refused. Griffiths' next move was to plot with a Bristol merchant called John Thorne, who was staying at his house, to come with him, on the pretext of buying the cargo, but they went with thirty armed men, who took the grain from Wolfall, and sold it openly in Barmouth.

In 1567, Morgan ab Ieuan accused John Bodfel of using Bardsey for piracy, and he started a case against him in the Star Chamber, but nothing came of it. John Bodfel faced a similar charge again in 1569, but, again, Bodfel, remained free and carried on trading with the pirates.

Piracy carried on into the 17th century in the area, and it is said that, in 1659, Bardsey pirates captured a total of twelve ships.

Dafydd Meirion (1950-2006): Welsh Pirates

'A Gift From Heaven'

Thomas Jones, born on Bardsey Island in 1877, has told of many a wreck forgotten on the mainland. He recalled a vessel laden with coal striking about a third of a mile north of the lighthouse. Like a gift from heaven, the coal lasted the islanders for many a year. The western cliffs of Bardsey have been claiming ships for at least 400 years and an enormous anchor of ancient vintage was found there towards the end of the last century. The Bibby Line screw steamer *Dalmatian*, 1,989 tons, built ten years earlier by Harland & Wolff, foundered in a storm near Bardsey in 1872. The Nefyn (Nevin) schooner *Reindeer*, of 97 tons, was abandoned off the island in 1874. The *Great Britain*, a Pwllheli schooner of 109 tones, was lost in the Sound in 1881. Another Pwllheli schooner, the *Jane and Eliza*, was lost there in 1885. Among the few names (and no dates) passed on by Thomas Jones was the *Leah*, of Scotland, which struck the western side of the island.

Ivor Wynne Jones: Shipwrecks of North Wales (1973)

Aristocratic Visitors

Curiosity induces many persons to visit this island almost every summer; but the grandest sight the present inhabitants ever witnessed, was at a visit of the proprietor, Lord Newborough, about eighteen years ago, accompanied by Lady Newborough, and several persons of distinction, in the whole to the number of about forty. This company embarked in fishing-smacks from Porthor, near Carreg Hall, in the parish of Aberdaron. On their arrival in the island, marquees were immediately pitched. The whole company dined in the open air; and, at the conclusion of their repast, all the inhabitants were assembled. The ensuing scene reminded a gentleman of my acquaintance, who was present, of what he had read respecting the inhabitants of some of the South-Sea islands. They were drawn up into a circle, and lady Newborough adorned the heads of the females with caps and ribbons, whilst lord Newborough distributed hats among the men. The nominal king and queen of the island were distinguished from the rest by an additional ribbon. Part of the day was occupied in strolling over the island, examining the creeks, and picking up shells, and the rest was spent in mirth and pleasantry. On the embarkation it was intended, being in the heat of summer, that the whole party should continue in the island till the next day. The ladies however, in the evening suddenly changed their resolution, and judiciously ordered the boats to be got ready. The rest of the company followed the example, and the night was spent, under the hospitable roof of Mr Thomas of Carreg, much more agreeably than could have been done in the island.

William Bingley (1774-1823): North Wales,
delineated from two excursions

Reflections

(Gerallt Jones spent a fortnight on Bardsey and during this period kept a journal. It was published in a limited edition.)

Monday, September 10th

The island has grown to be a part of my consciousness in a gradual shapeless way. I have given its contours and physical features comparitively little note. It is an atmosphere and a kind of cloak around me rather than a defined locality. And so this morning, when I wandered into the small enclosed ruin of St Mary's Abbey, it was the first time that I had really been aware of it, although it casts its shadow over my house, with its later Celtic cross, standing beside it, looming large alongside the path.

I cannot say that this remnant of grey wall calls up any particular visions in my mind. Whatever was the nature of monastic life on Bardsey, it was an inner strength that it must have developed, a resistance, a resilience, a tough interdependence that spread itself all over these fields, green from sweeping showers in the Dark Ages as they are today. It illuminated and informed every one of these four hundred and fifty acres; the stillness of their meditation was punctuated by the seal's mournful bark and the dry cry of gulls emphasised the silence. The most meaningful worship was the thankful seedtime and harvest that gave richness to these same fields, and their most meaningful protection and comfort was not any ediface of grey stone walls but the turbulent sea and the eloquent violent wind. They could climb to their ramparts on the slopes of Mynydd Enlli and lookout at the terrible dark world separated from them by the definitive barrier of Y Swnt; and from Pen Cristin on a clear day they could look south to that other embattled outpost behind the blue shadow of St David's Head. Standing within the shelter of the ruin, it seems no more directly relevant to the spirit that suffuses Bardsey than the fact that others have come to build houses here in this century, and that down by Maen Du there is a lighthouse that also stands out against wind and weather and shines into the dark.

Nevertheless, I felt this morning that the configurations of the place were in some way important. So I walked down from the abbey ruins, past Hendy, and wrote in my memory the feel and shape of things as I went. Everything stood out with a new definition, the solidity of the houses, Carreg and Plas Bach, their thick walls and geometric gardens, and the fade-away of the wet fields beyond, glistening with dew, stretching low to the little broken rocks where the seals lay. And on my left was a different picture, the steep sheep covered slopes, with Cristin within its siege-high walls and Ty Pella at the very end nestling in their shadow. The whole place seemed spacious, a big enough world, rich and full of minute variety. Crossing the tiny isthmus, past the landing-place, with the sea on either side licking submerged rocks, it had the impression of being new-made, unused, and I had the startling feeling that the grass I was looking at had never been trodden on. It was like a room with a new carpet, laid wall-to-wall for the first time. You stand at the door, momentarily afraid to spoil its texture, aware of its complete newness. Then the feeling passed and I crunched over dry sand towards the network of sea caves that finally face the stormy south. To create a way of life that was as confined as this, as structured and comprehensible, made a great deal of sense. It was a cosmos that could be recognised, treasured and kept in the mind, shaped and moulded and held all in one piece. It was a totality.

Each day the seals have been barking on the far shore, calling softly to each other through the quiet air and this afternoon for the first time I went close to them. I lay still on nearby rocks and watched. They were relaxed and at home, their great calm eyes unafraid as they rolled over in the sun and barked, out of no great necessity, but simply as a gentle statement of identity. They could see I was there, but they were unconcerned. They had no experience of human danger, no need to scuttle back into the welcoming sea. This strip of brown rock, camouflage brown, was theirs. But I could come and go as I pleased. They would tolerate me with no great interest, and watch me move off across the warm afternoon fields with equal indifference. I read and walked and loitered there all day with the seals for company. When I occasionally spoke to them I received a long still look of casual curiosity but nothing more. When I finally moved off in the evening light, yellow across the sea from the west, they didn't turn their heads or make any significant movement.

R. Gerallt Jones (1934-1999): Bardsey

Enlli

for Ceri when she was ten

We get to it through troughs and rainbows

flying and falling, falling and flying

rocked in an eggshell
over drowned mountain ranges.

The island swings towards us, slowly.

We slide in on an oiled keel,
step ashore with birth-wet, wind-red faces
wiping the salt from our eyes
and notice sudden, welling
quiet, and how here the breeze
lets smells of growing things
settle and grow warm, a host of presences
drowsing, their wings too fine to see.

There's a green track, lined with meadowsweet.
Stone houses, ramparts to the weather.
Small fields that run all one way
west to the sea, inviting feet
to make new paths to their own
discovered places.

After supper, lamplight
soft as the sheen of buttercups
and candle-shadow blossoms
bold on the bedroom wall.

Christine Evans

Enlli

No, I've never been there, with luck never shall,
Would be bored stiff in five minutes. All islands
Of this size are horribly alike, fit only
For sheep, saints and lighthousekeepers.
I've seen it at a distance from Aber prom
And that's as near, frankly, as I want to get.
I'm not surprised that hardly anybody lives there,
The gulls' gymanfa, the endless eisteddfod of eligugs,
The drooling chatter of the tide on the pebbles,
The moronic howl of the wind – well, I ask you.
Not, you'll say, much different from what goes on

On the mainland? Point taken. But
On top of all that, the traditions, paper flowers
Of crude fantasy, more than usually bogus
Even for this bloody country, if that's possible.
They had a king once, but he got drunk,
Well, that's kingly enough, but his crown
Was brass, he was appointed by the landlord.
And the gravestones of those twenty thousand saints
Thrown up in the age of faith by sheer ignorance –
Faith mostly spelt filth, futile pilgrimage
To no rational destination. I suppose that, really,
Is what Enlli is all about. You
My ancestors, were no fools who named it
One of the gates of heaven, outpost
Of the Kingdom of the Absurd, illogical,
Untidy, freak-out of geology, realm
Whose king had as good a title as some princes,
Almost, but not quite, nowhere, usually
Inaccessible but not always, utterly
Pointless but still marginally profitable,
Illusion, but anchored in rock.
If anybody prints this poem I'll send the price of it
To the fund to acquire Enlli for the nation.
God damn it, it is the Nation.

Harri Webb (1920-1994)

Beyond Llŷn

Beyond Lleyn there is a small island occupied by some
extremely devout monks, called the Coelibes or Colidei.

Either because of its pure air, which comes across the sea
from Ireland, or through some miracle occasioned by the
merits of the holy men who live there, the island has this
peculiarity, that no one dies there except in extreme old age,
for disease is almost unheard of. In fact, no one dies there at

all, unless he is very old indeed. In Welsh the place is called Ynys Enlli, and in the Saxon tongue Bardsey Island. The bodies of a vast number of holy men are buried there, or so they say, among them Daniel, Bishop of Bangor.

Giraldus Cambrensis (c.1146-1228):
The Journey Through Wales (translated by Lewis Thorpe)

A Hospitable Hand

. . . saints poured in here thickly from Brittany and Ireland, building cells and churches all along both the northern and the southern shore. The first of these, and the first in all North Wales was the abbey founded on the small and stormy island of Bardsey or Enlli, at the far end of the promontory. The destruction in 622, of Bangor Iscoed, near Wrexham, one of the greatest houses in Britain, by the Saxons, sent refugees from that noted massacre flying in panic to this remote sanctuary, in such numbers as to add to the importance it had already acquired. The very reasons indeed that now make localities remote were sometimes in ancient days the cause of contrary conditions. Here, for instance, Wales extended a hospitable hand far out into a sea that had greater terrors than it has for us, and it was eagerly clutched by the wandering saints and missionaries from the west, who braved the waves in fragile craft, and were glad enough to beach them on the sandy coves of Aberdaron and Porth Neigwl, and Abersoch. And Ynys Enlli, with its monastery became, above them all, a harbour of refuge, a sanctuary, and a mother of churches, dotting the coast of West Caernarvon, both north and south, with small shrines of stone and wood or even wickerwork, to be replaced in later days by walls more durable. Still more, however, was it as a place of pilgrimage that the island abbey became celebrated. Cures of body, and mind, and soul were to be had upon this lonely storm-washed rock. Above all it was a good thing to die here, and for generations, probably for centuries, men from all parts of the west limped and crawled and dragged themselves along the rude roads of Lleyn. Every church, upon both shores, became a shelter and a refuge to the pilgrims. Their endowments were charged with the task of providing food for those who came or went. By some legal oversight the farm of Pistyll, near Nevin, to this day goes tithe free, in consideration of furnishing provisions for this astonishingly obsolete purpose. Clynnog was the first stage from Carnarvon, and Llanaelliaiarn the second. Where the original walls of these old Lleyn churches in part or whole, survive, they are often scarred with the writing, and even with the rude illustrations, of the early British pilgrims, who sought passing shelter within them. Llanaelliaiarn, for example, was found covered with such inscriptions when the walls were scraped for its restoration not long ago. It is a cruciform church with oak rafters of unknown antiquity, some sedilia with fixed seats, and a rood screen of the fifteenth century, covered with many quaint devices. The old pews have been faithfully copied in the restoration and are framed not of solid wood, but of slender graceful rails, and this together with two churchwarden's chairs perched high, like thrones, upon either side of the aisle give the old building much originality. There is an old stone too, which the vicar greatly cherishes, bearing a Welsh inscription of unknown date signifying 'This is my seat and my grave'.

A. G. Bradley (1855-1945):
Highways and Byways of North Wales

Island in the Currents

The island is about 2 miles in circumference, contains few inhabitants and is rented from Lord Newborough. It was granted by Edward VI to his uncle Sir Thomas Seymour, and after his death to John Earl of Warwick. The late Sir John

Wynn purchased it from the late reverend Dr Wilson of Newark. Its spiritual concerns are at present under the care of a single rustic and once afforded, during life, an asylum to 20,000 saints; after death, graves to as many of their bodies. Well therefore might it be called Insula Sanctorum (*Isle of Saints*). But I must observe with Mr Fuller that 'it would be more facile to find graves in Bardseye for so many saints than saints for so many graves'. Dubritius, archbishop of Caer-leon, almost worn out with age, resigned his see to St David and retired here. According to the best account, he died in 612 and was interred on the spot but in after times his body was removed to Llandaf. The slaughter of the monks of Bangor, about the year 607, is supposed to have contributed to the population of the island. Not only the brethren who escaped but numbers of other pious Britons fled hither to avoid the rage of the Saxons.

The time in which the religious house was founded is very uncertain; it was probably before the retreat of Dubritius for something of that kind must have occasioned him to give the preference to this place. It seems likely to have been a seat of the Culdees or Colidei, the first religious recluses of Great Britain, who sought islands and desert places in which they might in security worship the true God. It was an abbey dedicated to St Mary, undergoing the common fate of others at the dissolution.

The Welsh named the island Ynys Enlli (*island in the currents*) from the fierce current which rages particularly between it and the main land. The Vikings called it Bardsey, probably from the bards who retired here preferring solitude to the company of invading foreigners. There are plenty of fish round the island and abundance of lobsters. We re-embarked from the rocks on the opposite side of the island to that on which we landed.

Thomas Pennant (1726-1798): A Tour in Wales

Ringing the Manxies

Little asthmatic banshees
in the night
you sweep in

over the great bulk of Mynydd Enlli

to where we are waiting
on the island's western edge
in the small low lying fields.

On the rocks seals lie snoring.

The night is full of your cries
palpably eerie,
as the four-petalled bloom

of the lighthouse beam

sweeps and slices in the dark.
The clamour of your music
its sibilant whistling creaking

is like no other sound in the world.

We have imagined you in your hundreds
upon hundreds, back at last from the Bay of Biscay
out at sea, rafting there

waiting for the safety of blackness.

The earth banks, the rabbit runs, silent till now,
cheep all at once with your chicks' ravenous welcome.
You are epic wanderers, manx shearwaters,

your very name a poem of tides and pearls.

Yet here, suddenly, you falter, tumbling
among furze, where capable hands catch you,
hold you, ring you, let you go.

You fall about us, a manna of bright birds.

Glenda Beagan

A Refuge

The noise began at around midnight, or that was when I woke to it. Birds were falling through the air above me, screaming while they fell, leaving long curved trails of sound as they plunged. I could hear them landing with soft thumps on the ground around me.

Every few seconds, one of the plunging birds and one of the turning lighthouse beams would coincide, vertical through lateral. I began to see them, here and there, momentarily outlined in the light – birds, with arrow-wings swept back from their little bomb-bodies, so that even as they disappeared, my eye retained an image of their streaking forms.

Shearwaters. Of course – they were shearwaters. Migratory, long-travelling, long-lived birds, which nested in burrows, and which waited until the cover of darkness before coming into land. Their name derives from their habit of gliding low over the water, wing-tips skidding the waves and striking droplets from them. The longest recorded wave-top glide of a Manx shearwater is one and a half miles. They are remarkable, too, for the distance of their pilgrimages. In a single day, they can cover as much as 200 miles. When the breeding season is over, obeying impulses beyond our cognition, the shearwaters of Enlli will fly thousands of miles to spend the rest of the year at sea in the South Atlantic.

Ynys Enlli, like so many of the islands and marshes on the east and west coasts of Britain, is a refuge for migrating birds. Hundreds of species stop off during their search for undisturbed feeding grounds. Tides and currents of birds, sweeping seasonally north and south, dispersing and returning, linking remote place to remote place.

Around two o'clock, the shearwaters settled. I lay in the quiet dark, watching the light beams turning silently above me, until I slipped back into sleep.

I woke to a still dawn. The sea, breathing quietly to my south, was pearly, with a light low mist upon it. The sky was pale with breaks of blue. The splash made by a black-backed gull diving fifty yards away sounded like a stone lobbed into the water nearby. I sat up, and saw that dozens of tiny dun-coloured birds were littering the rocks around me, making a high playground cheeping. Pipits. They gusted off when I moved.

I clambered down the shallowest side of the gulch, to the sharp angled rocks at the sea's edge, and washed my face in the idle water. On a rock ledge, I found and kept a heart-sized stone of blue basalt, beautifully marked with white fossils: coccoliths no bigger than a fingernail, the fine fanwork of their bodies still visible. I set a thin shell afloat, carrying a cargo of dry thrift heads. As I placed it on the water, it was sucked out away from my fingers on an invisible back eddy, bobbing with the gentle swell.

Robert MacFarlane: The Wild Places (2007)

Pen Llŷn

At the very tip is Enlli,
20,000 saints buried
out of archaeology's reach.

We are having a small summer,
haf bach we say.
A dense sun the end of October.

This afternoon mankind left,
and we are back at time's turning.
If it wasn't for the lighthouse wink
and a pale ghost ship
this could be the original garden.

On this lizard of land
I have forgotten everything.
My life shed along the roads,
worries in sharp bushes,
fears tumbling in a ditch.

You too have left life behind
to be here with me,
sitting, waiting for the sun
to paint us red and gold,
the two of us half-asleep
in this beautiful half-world.

Gwyn Parry

The Whittling

The island gods have turned inward,
fenced with water, bounded by the sea.

They duck their heads below the parapet
of wind and grow hard and nubbled

as heather roots, gorse twists, they shrink
into stone that pokes through bitten grass

clenched just below the surface.
They are marooned from their spawning grounds

in the icefields, bereft of rivers
that tumble through the lands,

cut off from the community of forests,
branches meeting each other in the dark.

They slip down to the shore to watch seals
nightly they envy their fluidity

and the zest of the invisible flocks
of shearwaters that pass with stuttering cries

inland, then out again through the gate of dawn.
Gods of the forest banished to driftwood scraps

have grown small and mean. He knew it,
the human visitor who took a knife

and chiselled this lump idly
released the god in the wood

with long thick head, a mind of dried tissue,
drilled eyes, a gouged grin

propped by a window: icon of isolation
made and abandoned for the next boat back

to wonder why it was called
forth, washed by changing light and voices

of passing strangers. Picked up, held
in the hand and made doll-like,

it whispers through its mouth-slit
be still, be still.

Hilary Llewelyn-Williams

Acknowledgements

We are indebted to the following for granting permission for work to be used in these pages.

Seren and the Estate of Brenda Chamberlain for 'Thick With Bones' from *Tide Race*.

Carcanet for *Welsh Incident* by Robert Graves and *Fires on Llŷn* by Gillian Clarke.

Glenda Beagan and Honno for 'Ringing the Manxies' from *Vixen*.

John Fuller for 'Walking Below Carn Guwch' and 'Nant Gwrtheyrn' which appeared in *The Mountain in the Sea*, published by Secker and Warburg.

Seren for the use of work by Ruth Bidgood, Christine Evans, Mike Jenkins, Steve Griffiths and Hilary Llewelyn-Williams.

The Estate of Harri Webb for the use of his translation of 'Young Fellow From Llŷn'.

Professor Joseph P. Clancy for his translation of 'Aberdaron' by Albert Evans-Jones (Cynan).

Gomer for the extracts from R. Gerallt Jones' *A Place in the Mind* (2004).

The Estate of R. Gerallt Jones for 'Reflections' from *Bardsey* by R. Gerallt Jones (Tern Press 2004) and the same authors' translation of his poem 'A Funeral in Llŷn'.

Michael Ponsford for 'Ffynnon Fair'.

Gomer for extracts from *Across the Straits* by Kyffin Williams.

Grahame Davies for his translation of 'Sunset Over Llŷn' by Sion Aled which is included in *The Bloodaxe Book of Modern Welsh Poetry* (2003).

Alun Llwyd for 'The Moons of Llŷn', translated by Joseph P. Clancy, which appears in *The Bloodaxe Book of Modern Welsh Poetry* (2003).

Mike Jenkins for his translation of 'The Living Spring' by Moses Glyn Jones, which is included in *The Bloodaxe Book of Modern Welsh Poetry* (2003).

Bridge Books for permission to use two extracts from *A History of Caernarfonshire* by A. H. Dodd (1968).

Gwynedd Archive for 'Holyhead or Porthdinllaen' from *Packet to Ireland* (1984).

Jan Morris for extracts from *Wales: Epic Views of a Small Country* (Viking).

University of Wales Press for 'A Matter of Life and Death' from *Presenting Saunders Lewis* edited by Alun R. Jones and Gwyn Thomas (1983).

Paul Henry for 'Welsh Incident'.

The Estate of Harri Webb for his poem 'Enlli'.

Gomer for 'Island of the Blest' from *Welsh Country Essays* (1997).

Y Lolfa for 'A Convenient Place for Pirates' from *Welsh Pirates* by Dafydd Meirion (2004).

Granta for an extract from *The Wild Places* by Robert Macfarlane (2007).

The Orion Publishing Company and the Estate of R. S. Thomas for use of the following poems: 'Pen Llŷn', 'Abersoch', 'The Moon in Llŷn' and 'Ffynnon Fair'.

Joseph P. Clancy for his translation of 'Penyberth' by Gwynn ap Gwilym which appears in *The Bloodaxe Book of Modern Welsh Poetry* (2003).

Gwyn Parry for the use of two poems.